AF407162

Points of Light

by CAMERON WALKER

WINNER OF
THE TAMAQUA AWARD

Hidden River Arts offers The Tamaqua Award, a prize of $1000 and publication by Hidden River Press, an imprint of Hidden River Publishing, for an original collection of essays.

Hidden River Arts is an interdisciplinary arts organization dedicated to supporting and celebrating the unserved artists among us, particularly those outside the artistic and academic mainstream.

Points of Light

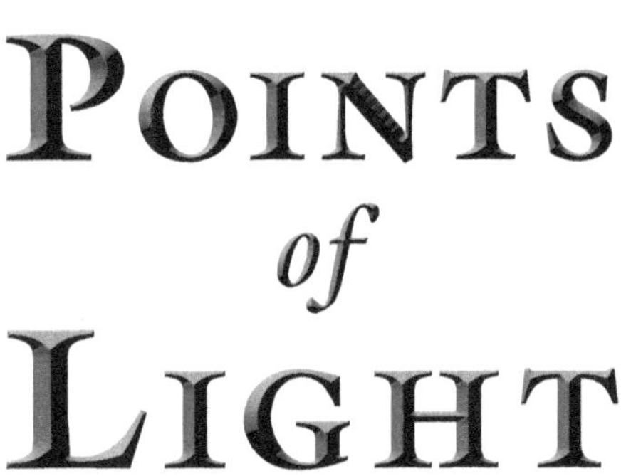

*Curious Essays on Science,
Nature, and Other Wonders
Along the Pacific Coast*

CAMERON WALKER

HIDDEN RIVER PRESS
Philadelphia 2024

Copyright © 2024 Cameron Walker

All rights reserved

No part of this book may be used or reproduced in any manner whatsoever without written permission, except in the case of brief quotations embodied in critical articles and reviews.

Without in any way limiting the author's and publisher's exclusive rights under copyright, any use of this publication to "train" generative artificial intelligence (AI) technologies to generate text is expressly prohibited. All rights to license uses of this work for generative AI training and development of machine learning language models are strictly reserved.

Cover design: Lesley MacLean
Interior design: P. M. Gordon Associates, Inc.
Interior landscape image by Freepik

Library of Congress Control Number: 2021952615

ISBN 979-8-9854317-0-4

HIDDEN RIVER PRESS
Philadelphia, Pennsylvania

For my parents,
M.W. and G.K.L.

Contents

LOOKING UP

Auditing Astronomy Class

I'M NOT SURE exactly where this story begins, but maybe it's here: one summer, my mom decided to take an astronomy class. She had taken drama and philosophy classes through the Osher Lifelong Learning Institute at UC Berkeley and audited a history of theater course on campus. She'd heard about a particular astronomy class aimed at non-science majors; the professor, Alex Filippenko, had won all sorts of teaching awards. She emailed him to see if it was okay for her to sit in—it was—and then convinced a few friends to join her.

Maybe what I should say next is that my mom has never been very interested in science. I actually didn't know how much she didn't like it until I asked. In college, she fulfilled her science requirement with comparative anatomy, a class that required dissecting frogs and cats. "I hated the smell of formaldehyde," she said. "Dinner was right after that. I just hated it."

Astronomy had also gotten on her bad list. "Whenever I saw something in the paper about a comet, a supernova—I just didn't read it. I thought, I'm never going to understand this anyway."

This class had no formaldehyde, just a professor who has enough astronomy-themed T-shirts to cover three afternoons a week for a whole semester without repeating a shirt. Before each class, he played a piece of music that related to the theme of the lecture, from "Clair de Lune" to "popular stuff, like by Moby," my mom said.

That's how I first heard about what was going on in class. My mom called one day and asked if I knew what shepherd moons are. I didn't (although I did know the song by Enya), so she explained.

I wished I had my pen and notebook with me, so I could have written down exactly what she said. But I'm not sure I could have captured how it felt to hear. Her voice had the same combination of cheeriness and awe usually reserved for plays, mystery novels, and British period dramas—but there was something else in it, too. Shepherd moons, she told me, were moons near the rings around planets. These moons can shape a ring with the force of their own gravity.

The next time I asked her about the class, I had a pen handy. I can't totally decipher my notes—partly because I was tucking the phone against my chin, propping a baby against my side with a forearm, and scribbling on the back of an envelope on top of the piano, but mainly because it felt odd to take notes while talking to my mom. But here's a sampling:

"gamma ray bursts"

"black holes are the warping of space and time"

"evaporating black holes"

And the last line: "I know enough that I look at the world differently."

That's what she said every time she talked about the class—that knowing more about the stars had made the world around her change.

She told me it's because of the professor. For Halloween, he dressed up as a black hole and, with the help of his own kids, tossed Mars Bars and Starbursts to the students in the lecture hall. He swung a doughnut on a string to demonstrate centripetal force. According to a report from one of his students, he once even broke a rib in class when he jumped on to a skateboard from a desk.

My mom said he connects astronomy to everyday life. When Pluto got demoted as a planet, some people were upset. Sometimes, he told the class, you just have to get over it. Maybe you didn't get an A on a test. Maybe you broke up with a girlfriend. Maybe you're still orbiting the sun, even though you aren't part of a special club anymore (which my mom now knows by the mnemonic "My Very Educated Mother Just Served Us Nothing").

I listened to one of Dr. Filippenko's lectures online. This one was about asteroids, and while I know it's not the same as hearing it in person, I did start to understand what she meant. Near the end of the lecture, he moves from the basics of asteroids to talk about how an earth-wide crisis, like an impending collision, might someday bring people together. In the recording, you can hear the students breaking into applause. The sound of it sent me about the rest of my earthbound day still feeling like there was a hand cupped under my heart.

My mom said she's not always sure she understands exactly what he's saying, but she feels like she could. She might take the class again the next time he teaches it. She started watching episodes of *NOVA*. My mom read to me from her notes: we are made of stardust, that every atom inside us is made of elements from exploding stars. She told me that there's a meteor shower coming up. She couldn't remember which one.

This was at the end of the most recent email I got from her about the class:

this quote from Steve Weinberg (don't know who he is):

<The effort to understand the universe is one of the few things that lifts human life a little above the level of farce, and gives it some of the grace of tragedy>

Can't remember why I wrote that down, but I liked it.

I like it, too. And now I know what I was trying to explain about her voice, just like I know where this story should begin. It's not tragedy at all, just grace.

Window Seat

AT 3 A.M., a quiet settles like fog around the neighborhood, freckled by a few bursts of sound: the whistle of an incoming train, sea lion barks from a far-off buoy, the deep buzz of fishing boats. Sometimes, an acoustical trick even carries the rush of incoming waves. Occasionally, a single too-loud bird coughs out a call, then silences itself. I imagine that it's a youngster, unable to stop from bursting into laughter, with the parents giving it the avian equivalent of the look that means *pull yourself together right now or else.*

For the past few weeks, I've found myself sitting in the middle of the night in front of a one-square-foot hole in the wall where a window used to be. There's not a clock in the room, but when an engine rallies down the dark street, followed by the thwack of the newspaper on the sidewalk, dawn is still more than an hour away.

A square foot doesn't seem like much of a view. But one night, a star appeared: extremely bright, familiar, and totally unidentifiable without its surrounding constellation, at least for me. I couldn't get up—the baby in my arms was drifting in a space that was not quite sleep. So I just watched the star and noticed its warble. The light seemed to change from pale blue to pale green to white, although I wondered if the colors were scraps leftover from a dream.

The first book about writing that I read was Anne Lamott's *Bird by Bird.* At first, I tried to employ her advice—break things into small pieces, ignore the voices in your head—but over the years, I let much of it fall away because I got too busy writing, or at least doing the busy work that accompanies it.

One of the pieces of advice that I hadn't recalled until just recently was the one-inch picture frame on her desk. When she's scattered, all she has to do—she tells herself—is write as much as she can see through that tiny space.

Just an inch. Just a foot. Just one molecule. Just one star. But within those spaces—I'd forgotten it until now—so much is contained.

Others have done wonderful things with a limited view. Elisabeth Tova Bailey, bedridden with a debilitating illness, could do little more than observe the small snail in her bedside terrarium. Watching and caring for the snail not only helped renew her sense of purpose, but also allowed her to draw the connections between the snail's life history and her own place in nature in *The Sound of a Wild Snail Eating.* My blue hours in the rocking chair will be over too soon, but I don't want to lose what I've relearned here—that focusing quietly on a single thing can actually expand the view.

Over the past week, the view has changed. Slowly, slowly, the stars wheel around. And then one night there is something I do recognize: Orion's three-star belt. A while later the bright star reappears. I should have recognized it earlier—come on, it's the brightest star in the sky, it's the Dog Star, it's the name of the person who makes Harry Potter feel like he has a family at last. Just as I do now, sitting here in the rocker. "That's Sirius," I say to the baby. And even if someday I don't remember its name, I'll still remember the night we saw this star together.

Moonstruck

THE EAGLE OWLS began to call at dusk, right around the time the full moon started to rise in the east. Watching and listening were the ecologist Vincenzo Penteriani and his crew. They would be up all night, trying to learn more about the behavior of these owls, Europe's largest, with wings that could spread across a king-size bed.

On this particular full-moon night, Penteriani realized that there would be a lunar eclipse. As soon as the shadow of the Earth covered the moon, the owls fell silent.

Scientists had long thought that nocturnal animals primarily used sound to communicate. But one evening, Penteriani caught sight of a male owl through his binoculars, just after sunset. With each call, a previously hidden patch of white feathers flashed along the owl's throat: a visual cue, the researcher later found, that was key to the species' mating strategy. And on nights of brightest moonlight, these calls and flashes increase.

Nearly a third of vertebrates, and more than 60 percent of invertebrates, are active at night; the full moon is the brightest object for most of their waking hours. About two weeks after the moon's brightest phase, the new moon will rise at sunrise and set with the sun, leaving the entire night starlit. The whole cycle runs about 29.5 days from new moon to new moon, and ecologists such as Penteriani, now a researcher with the Spanish National Research Council, want to know how this shifting pattern of lunar light and darkness shapes animals' lives.

In our world of street lights and headlamps and blinding motion sensors, we—at least, I—no longer rely on the moon. Often, I don't even remember that it's up there: it seems to surprise me appearing from behind a tree, its light a shock when I wake from a dream.

Yet the moon has always been in our stories, whether nursery rhymes or darker tales. Clouds unfurl from the face of the full moon and a man becomes a werewolf. Vampires lurk, magic potions burble, bats take wing. Given these tales of night terrors, we might think that predators prefer the full moon's light to stalk their prey. But when the ecologists Laura Prugh and Christopher Golden surveyed the behavior of 59 nocturnal mammals, they found that most carnivores and insectivores became less active under the brightest moon phases. Primates seemed to be the only group that was consistently more active under the full moon.

Without electric lighting, that applies to us, too. A few centuries ago, anyone who wanted to move about at night depended on the phase of the moon. By the 17th century, those in cities relied on almanacs to plan their night-time journeys, writes the historian A. Roger Ekirch in *At Day's Close: Night in Times Past.* In autumn, farmers used the bounty of light from the harvest moon to reap the season's crops late into the night. Thieves and other human predators sometimes refused to work nights when the "tattler" in the sky might give them away.

For millennia, humans have wondered if the moon pulls at us with something more than its reflected light. Pliny the Elder observed that, in combination with the sun, the moon draws up the tides. Pliny and his compatriots also argued that this lunar force—now known as gravity—pulls on the moisture in our bodies, within our watery brains. The full moon's drag was thought to cause everything from epilepsy to "lunacy." These days, a few studies have linked human health and behavior with the full moon, but more have refuted the connection: Gravity's effect on us is known to be so tiny that it wouldn't sway our aquatic inner reaches, even during the tidal extremes known as spring tides, around the new and full moons, when the sun and the moon both exert their gravitational pull in concert.

But it's hard to shake the feeling that something which looms so large in our night sky, and in the firmament of our imaginations, could be a simple satellite—particularly when its shifting light shapes the lives of so many of our fellow travelers, the creatures of the night.

Although we might be drawn to the showy shine of a full moon, the vanishing of this light as it starts to wane could be just as powerful. At the full moon, the Earth stands between the moon and the sun, and the view of our long-time companion is that of a brightly lit coin. During the following nights, as the moon circles back toward the sun, that coin slowly shrinks, yet the sky seems much darker than just the dwindling light would allow. And it is: the moon rises about 50 minutes later each evening, carving a channel of darkness between the sun dropping below the horizon and the moon appearing.

It's this channel that can be travelled by predators, and might also have created our lingering fears about the full moon. In Tanzania, the sun sets by 7 p.m. throughout the year. But people still cook outdoors, greet neighbors, walk to get water, often well after nightfall.

The lions here are less likely to hunt under a full moon. But as that moon wanes and the evenings darken, these hungrier lions might encounter not just their traditional prey but people still out in the open. Researchers have found that lion attacks on humans were most likely in the 10 days *after* the full moon.

About seven days after the full moon, it becomes a semicircle of light called the third quarter moon. This moon rises close to midnight, too late for many daytime creatures to see. The stars take over. Penteriani's eagle owls quieten. Another week, and we can no longer see its illumination, even if we stay up all night.

When the moon passes through our sky during the daytime, rising at sunrise and setting at sunset, some cultures call it the dark moon, others the new moon. In some calendars, the new moon is when the first slice of returning crescent is seen. Whatever the name, when the moon passes between us and the sun, these nights of lowest light allow other creatures to appear.

The waters of the Philippines are central to the Coral Triangle, a region of the western Pacific with hundreds of coral reefs and thousands of species of reef fish. Traditional fishermen on Samal Island bring the catch home from the surrounding waters: with 31 fishing villages on the island's coast, it can be difficult for marine biologists such as Arthur Bos to find out how many are being caught from which species.

Over a period of two years, Bos and a colleague made more than 100 visits to Peña Plata, the island's largest fish market, where small stalls display everything from red snapper to mangoes, and customers wheedle the vendors for an extra fillet. At first, Bos simply recorded which species appeared at the market in hopes of learning more about the Davao Gulf.

But soon he noticed a pattern: during the full moon and the days that followed, reef fish were difficult, even impossible, to find. During the new moon, you could buy plenty of snappers, groupers, parrotfish, and other coral reef species— more than 80 percent of the stalls sold reef fish.

The dark nights around the new moon cue nocturnal fish to leave their shelters among the reef, says Bos, now at the American University in Cairo. Under cover of darkness, these fish are less likely to be seen by aquatic predators—and the fishermen use this to their advantage, stalking the fish with spears and, sometimes, with electric torches.

The dark nights of the new moon also call land species out of their shelters. In Spain's Doñana National Park, rabbits watch out for both Iberian lynx and red fox prowling the scrubland. Penteriani and his crew put radio tags on dozens of animals of all three species and followed their night-time movements throughout the lunar cycle.

He had guessed that rabbits might stay close to their burrows during the full moon, which they did. Around the new moon, they hopped further from home, using direct movements to cross long, exposed distances. The rabbits' behavior during the lunar cycle might be a response to changing predator behavior, as well to the available light—their travelling urges came a few days *after* the new moon, and there was also a delay after the full moon before they kept closest to home.

During a new moon in other parts of the world, coyotes howl as a group. European badgers pee more. Bad weather and eclipses serve as transient dark moons; one species of nightjar has been seen to stop its moonlight foraging when heavy clouds blanketed the moon. And then, just as the night seems as if it will never brighten, a glimpse of a crescent appears in the west just after the sun goes down.

Now we think of the word crescent as the fingernail shape, but in Latin *crescens* referred to the waxing of the moon: a crescendo of reflected light. About seven days after the new moon, we see a quarter moon again. If you were to look down at your thumb, you might find a pale quarter moon at the base of your nail. It's called the lunula and formed while you were still in the womb.

Gabriele Cozzi, at the University of Zurich, started thinking of the moon in northern Botswana, where he was studying how lions, cheetahs, African wild dogs, and hyenas used the landscape. It had been thought that these species divided themselves across a 24-hour day to avoid crossing paths: lions and hyenas were known to hunt primarily at night, while wild dogs and cheetahs were considered daytime hunters. Taking shifts makes sense, particularly for smaller predators: lions will kill wild dogs and cheetahs. Hyenas steal their hard-earned catches.

Cozzi was looking mainly at how these animals behaved at dawn and dusk. After a few months, however, he found that cheetahs and wild dogs seemed to be more active at night than he'd imagined. Every 30 days or so, the tiny accelerometers on the animals' radio collars would show a burst of activity. Cozzi wondered what happened every month to jolt them into action. Then it came to him: "It has to do with moonlight."

He found that both wild dogs and cheetahs started picking up their activity levels at night once half the moon was illuminated. Lions and hyenas, on the other hand, didn't seem to change their night-time hunting patterns, regardless of what moon passed overhead.

Cheetahs are famously speedy hunters; wild dogs are no slouches either, running down their prey to exhaustion at 50 miles an hour or more—a difficult feat in full darkness through the thickets of the Okavango Delta. Moonlight illuminates the hunt, and, while the transmitters couldn't track how successful their chases were, Cozzi saw wild dogs sleeping with large bellies the morning after a brightly lit night.

As the moon waxes from first quarter through gibbous (or more-than-half full) to full, Cozzi's wild dogs and cheetahs increase their nocturnal activity; by the full moon, 40 percent of their typical day's "work" is done at night. One species of lunar-loving nightjars, known after their birdcall as whip-poor-wills, hatch in the few days following the new moon: in the following days, when the nestlings start demanding more food, their parents will be able to hunt under the bright moonlight. Gibbous is also a word for hunchback, and as the moon grows, it rounds its shoulders until it rolls into a great ball of light.

Oh, the full moon. It seems to bring so much light and we give it so much more to bear symbolically. We sing about the romance of moondances, and worry that the full moon might make us, or the world around, crazy. Even Penteriani calls his research, which has involved more than eight years and thousands of hours chasing animals in the darkness, "lunatic." Under the full moon, young eagle owls start to leave their home nests, using the light to seek out new territory and potential prey. Older eagle owls emit their haunting hoots, flashing their white throats at each other from high perches.

Other creatures shy away from the light. The image of a colony of bats winging its way across the round moon is iconic, but many bat species become less active around the full moon. While reef fish keep themselves hidden, a fisherman in the Philippines might leave his spear at home and gather sea urchin, shellfish and sea cucumbers instead.

The full moon's link to romance, at least of the invertebrate kind, is evident along Australia's Great Barrier Reef, where researchers and divers flock each austral spring to see the symphony of corals releasing their gametes at once, a few days after the full moon. The spectacle, people say, looks like drifting underwater snow, pink and yellow and white.

When researchers looked more closely, they found that a gene encoding a coral cryptochrome, a protein that's sensitive to blue light, begins expressing itself much more on full-moon nights. Five days later, the corals begin to spawn. The lunar cycle cues corals to release their gametes at the same time, making successful reproduction more likely. In other species, the Moon ties into other environmental cues that aid in creating the next generation—whether cues about food availability, as for the dark-hatching whip-poor-will, or about the tides.

Researchers have even started to find animals that continue to find food, and each other, in time with the Moon's phases, even when they can't see its light. This circalunar clock might be ticking in co-ordination with an animal's 24-hour circadian timepiece to help it survive.

Galápagos marine iguanas travel from their resting spots, leaving as much as four hours ahead of time, to arrive at the shoreline to graze for algae at low tide; the ones that arrive the earliest fare the best. They do this even when they can't see the ocean and when their dark/light cycles are interrupted, suggesting to biologists that an interior clock, based on the tides and the underlying lunar cycle guides these iguanas.

Other marine species, too, seem to be able to track the moon's phases even without its light. The gonads of the marine bristle worm *Platynereis dumerilii* mature in time with the lunar cycle; it performs its mating dance and releases gametes around the new moon. Worms raised in the lab under a mimicked lunar cycle mature and reproduce in synchrony with this cycle, even once the light treatment stopped, suggesting that the moon's light locks in the clock's rhythm, which can then run even without the moon in sight.

Many of us live in places where it's hard to see the light of the moon, and many of the connections between ourselves and the moon that have been passed down through generations have been discounted, or at least called into question. So when a group of chronobiologists in Switzerland sat at a riverside bar in Basel one full-moon night, and started wondering if the moon might affect people's sleep, the idea was a bit of a joke.

They'd done a study several years earlier, in which 17 young and 16 older volunteers had come into the sleep lab for more than three days at a time. They were completely sealed off from any cues about light, dark and time of day. Everything from the volunteers' brainwave activity to their levels of melatonin was measured.

At the time, they were trying to find out more about how age affected sleep. Now, under the full moon, they started thinking that they might take another look at their data to see if people's sleep and other biological rhythms were affected by the lunar cycle.

The researchers—led by Christian Cajochen, who directs the Centre for Chronobiology at the University of Basel—waited more than two years to publish their results, primarily to check and recheck their analyses, but in part to avoid any hype about how the moon and the people beneath it might be entangled.

Because they did see entanglement. When volunteers in

their study, whether old or young, stayed in the lab during the three or four days around the full moon, they spent five minutes longer trying to fall asleep than those who stayed in the lab during other times of the lunar month. Their full-moon sleep was 20 minutes shorter; they felt less rested, and slept 30 percent less deeply than those who visited the lab during other times. They couldn't see the moon, and the researchers hadn't even noted the moon phase at the time.

Is there anything else that would make someone sleep this poorly? "It's called growing old," says Anna Wirz-Justice, a chronobiologist and professor emeritus at the University of Basel, who worked on the study.

Wirz-Justice and her colleagues are still waiting for other labs to replicate their results so that they feel confident about their findings. But their work suggests that humans, too, might have a circalunar clock—although finding this might prove difficult, as the powerful circadian cycle could be masking smaller lunar effects.

Multiple biological clocks could be governing our waking and sleeping lives, in ways we haven't yet determined. For every study that negates the link between the moon and birth, a midwife or obstetrician will swear that they've seen more babies born during the moon's brightest phase. My friend who's an emergency room nurse—my rational, dependable friend—steels herself for full-moon nights of accidents, injuries, people in distress. She says it's one of the few patterns she and her co-workers can depend on.

Maybe our stories of the moon run too deep. In the past, many of us were more connected to the moon: maybe we still carry this cultural history with us, even if evidence of biological effects has faded. Or these clocks might be quietly counting the hours somewhere beneath our screens and lamps, our false moons.

Or maybe it's just easier to believe in the eventful moon-lit nights that we accumulate throughout our own lives. No matter whether other researchers confirm the results from Basel, I will still blame my restless nights on the moon, because otherwise this restlessness might mean I am growing old.

Perhaps we're looking for patterns in the wrong places, while the bright moon goes on calling prey out from their hideouts, telling the corals that the time is ripe, letting the owls sing their eerie song. Perhaps the moon affects our lives, in ways that are more subtle, more resonant.

In wintertime where I live, the full moon rises over the mountains. You can see it first as a small patch of sky, a little bit brighter than the rest. Then a small line of light traces the edge of the jagged crest, then a whole piece of moon. Finally, the full moon hangs there, as if it could roll along the ridges and plunk into the ocean below. On full-moon nights, a small crowd gathers at the bluff before dusk. They set up cameras and telescopes, murmuring to each other, checking watches.

If we have an internal clock run by the moon, it's true that we might not hear it tick as loudly as those whose waking lives are spent in the dark. But look at all those people on the bluff. As the moon emerges, their voices quiet. They lean closer to their companions, they take deep breaths and gaze at this great, reflected light. Something in us is ticking, even if it's only the beat of our hearts.

Points of Light

COMING DOWN from Gaviota Pass, it's the ocean I see first. But I look past the waves and ignore the distant Channel Islands, searching for the landmarks on the horizon that tell me I'm really home.

They are not the sort of islands you might imagine. They don't have beautiful names like Anacapa and Santa Rosa, or national parks, or blue whales or rare foxes. The things that make me feel most at home are the oil rigs.

Twenty platforms, gray and stork-legged from the shore, sit in the Santa Barbara Channel. In 1969, one dumped 100,000 barrels of crude into these waters. The spill ignited a local movement that some consider the start of nationwide interest in the environment.

Even though I know I shouldn't, there is still something in me that loves how the rigs look after sunset, when they become little oases of orange sparkle on the dark sea. When I fly, my eyes search for these other islands, too, as we bank and straighten out, bound for the runway. But I've always been slightly embarrassed by my appreciation of them.

So I was relieved when another writer confessed that he'd always been fond of the rigs, too. He told me he was "a sucker for big industrial engineering," able to admire a structure's mechanical splendor even if its purpose was not as noble as he wished.

I don't think it's the engineering that attracts me, though. I used to paddle outrigger canoes, and one of our races took us closer to the rigs than I'd ever been before. As they loomed larger, their appeal diminished. Their gray bulk became a paler blue, their legs appeared both more massive and more spindly. Frightening and fragile at once—or perhaps that was just how I felt in the boat, as I carefully positioned my body so we wouldn't capsize.

The first time I remember seeing the rigs, I was sticky from a long drive and had cracked the windows to get a breath of ocean air. And then there they were, the smallest of lights and something cracked inside me, and was remade.

I wonder if the lights of the rigs serve as my substitute for stars. We can see stars here, of course, the familiar constellations of the Big Dipper and Orion. But our nights are often soaked with fog, and my house is close to others and to a brightly lit stadium. The only time I remember the sky filling with the salty scatter of the Milky Way was for a few hours after a storm, when the sky had cleared but the power in our neighborhood was still out.

But can I really love these distant, deceitful, industrial gleams as much as people love stars? I wrote to William Kelly, now a psychologist at Neumann University in Pennsylvania, about whether there could be some connection between the night sky and these earthbound imitations.

Kelly has come up with a word for the love of the night sky: *noctcaelador*. For the past 10 years, he's been looking at how to measure this idea, and also studied how and why the love of the night sky might develop.

He hasn't studied oil rigs or other artificial glimmers, but

I asked him to guess, and so he did. He speculated that the attraction might be hardwired in our brains. Throughout the ages, the night sky has inspired everything from calendars to religion, he said. Along the way, the human psyche may have started relying on and identifying with the points of light above our heads, our eyes using them as anchors in the endless expanse of sky. "Maybe unconsciously, when we see a beautiful array of lights, some ancient part of ourselves gets activated," he said, "just like it does when we're looking at the night sky."

There is another place I feel I belong. It's a camp in the Sierra that my family started visiting when I was six. In college, I worked on the camp staff. This summer, I returned for the first time in more than a decade, with my own young family in tow. Everything essential was unchanged—the butterscotch smell of the Jeffrey pine, the swirls of dust on the paths, the burble of the creek, and particularly, the easy camaraderie among the people there.

Yet there was something missing, something just beyond the edge of my vision. I chalked it up to the difference between being a carefree kid and being the parent of carefree kids hopped up on bug juice and marshmallows and mountain air.

On the last night, everyone went to bed early, and my husband and I sat outside the tent. The moon had been full at the beginning of the week, and this was the first time we'd really looked up to the patch of sky between the treetops.

There they were: all the stars that I'd grown up with. And I felt the same way that I do when I see the rigs at last. *Home*, something inside me said. *I'm home again.*

View from Above

MOST OF THE PEOPLE I followed on Facebook were friends from high school and college, so I usually saw photos of kids, drinking establishments, and scenic shots of the West. But in spring 2013, I caught on to what 710,000 Twitter followers and 219,354 Facebook friends (as of one Tuesday that April) already knew—and started following Col. Chris Hadfield, a Canadian astronaut who had been living aboard the International Space Station since mid-December 2012 and became the space station's commander in March.

Hadfield had become a social media superstar, of the best kind: shilling not for himself, but for space. He posted delightful YouTube videos that answer questions I didn't even know I had: *How do astronauts sleep? How do they cut their fingernails? Why do they make their sandwiches with tortillas? How do they cry?* (Some answers: Tethered in sleeping bags, without a pillow, their arms floating up. Near an air duct, so the clippings don't float away. Bread is too crumbly. They can't cry, really—their tears form a big ball and never fall.)

He answered questions from around the world on Reddit. He and another famous space commander, William Shatner of the starship Enterprise, had a live chat. He tweeted and posted gorgeous photos of the Earth from on high every day. He had an April Fool's Day encounter with a cartoon alien. He sang a song from space with the Barenaked Ladies' Ed Robertson. His tweets navigated a fine balance between aw-shucks and awestruck. He could see 16 sunrises a day.

All the zero-gravity humor and the instant contact with space might have given me a false sense of closeness with my new favorite astronaut. I was particularly reminded of this when reading an essay by the commander's son Evan, who was the on-the-ground force behind Hadfield's extensive social media presence. In *The Globe and Mail*, he wrote, *So my fear isn't really that my dad is going to die. Everyone's dad dies. My fear is that he won't die once but a thousand times, with a million people talking about him as though he were a concept instead of a man.*

At the time, I felt like this connection, mirage or not, could help me, too. The photos I saw of Earth through Hadfield's eyes seemed more meaningful, somehow, than what I read in the news. Forest fires in Mongolia and Australia from above were more devastating; a pit mine in a green landscape became a deeper scar. But now, with Hadfield returned safely home, I find myself thinking about his son's words, too, as much as I do about the view from above. My own dad died once, and once felt like more than enough. How would it be to have to relive it over and over again, to feel like somehow you must comfort others as you found your own way through grief?

I don't know how to reconcile this with the view of the world that he and others have given us, a change in perspective—then and now—that shows us the world as we hope it could be. In his photos, Washington, D.C. and Jerusalem look peaceful, united by illumination, while a mining town in Kazakhstan is starkly beautiful. And maybe that's the thing—the photos show the beauty that we can't recognize when it's right in front of us.

I have never had more love and respect for our planet than I do now, seeing it this way. —Chris Hadfield (@Cmdr_Hadfield) April 22, 2013.

I haven't always been fascinated with space or space travel (a deficiency that might run in the family), and I've been known to get Neil Armstrong confused with another famous Neil. So when I saw another of Hadfield's posts on Facebook, it took me a moment to understand what he was talking about:

Talked with Neil Young tonight, he in his hybrid 1959 Lincoln, [me] in a spaceship. Discussed Earth ecology & writing music. A heart of gold.

I do not know how to look at the world from above. I don't even know how to look at the world through another person's eyes, as much as I would like to. But maybe that's the thing to look for, whatever the view: The heart. The gold.

Ocean View

Psyche and the Seashore

Years ago, I lived among trees. The world was lush and quiet, populated by deer and wild turkeys, outlined by ferns and running creeks. It sounds idyllic, and in many ways, it was. And then I moved to the California coast. Here, as soon as I get within sensory reach of the ocean—whether it's to smell the salt air, hear the boom-hiss of breaking waves, or scan out to the distant horizon—a deep tide of ease rises in me, bringing both clarity and contentment.

Not everyone feels this way. For some, the same ricochet of water on sand inspires mild panic; the open water stretches into a yawn of loneliness, not comfort. So what draws so many of us to gaze out over the waves—and sends others to higher ground for the company of conifers or the shelter of steep mountains?

I started thinking about this after reading about a recent series of studies linking people's personalities to the kinds of landscapes they prefer. Psychologist Shigehiro Oishi worked with groups of students at the University of Virginia (UVA), surveying them to see where they would like to go to seek solitude, and where they'd prefer to be when socializing with friends. Three-quarters of the 220-plus students picked the beach for group activity. For quieter retreats, students split more evenly between mountains and ocean.

Oishi also looked at large personality studies and sorted the results geographically: residents of states with the highest mountains and the most mountains tended to be more introverted than those who lived elsewhere. Among the possible explanations, he wondered if geography itself—the sheltered protection of mountains, or the broad, open spaces that you might find at the seashore—could actually cause people to become more extroverted or introverted.

But when he tested the idea on groups of UVA students, he found that his introverted subjects remained reticent no matter whether they were in an open space or a sheltered environment. The same pattern was true of more gregarious individuals: environment did little to change their nature. While his research on the connection between personality and landscape is still in its early stages, he says our personalities may guide us to seek out particular landscapes; perhaps, Oishi told attendees at a psychology meeting one February, "introverts like me choose mountainous places like Charlottesville."

I'm an introvert, too, but for me the wide-open view of the sea is often more comforting than being in the mountains; the refuge Oishi and others may find there sometimes seems too close and confining. So what might draw me to the ocean, instead? The psychology of introverts seems to cast some light on this. In her book, *Quiet*, writer Susan Cain talks about how introverts are particularly attuned to what's happening around them. She points to research like that of developmental psychologist Jerome Kagan and his colleagues, who looked at how infants react to new things in their environments. The researchers found that babies who were especially responsive to new things—from unfamiliar voices to bursting balloons—were more likely to become quieter, more cautious teenagers. In introverts, the amygdala, the area of the brain that processes emotions, is more sensitive to stimuli, too, so anything new sets off a flush of reactions, from a higher heart rate to more cortisol in the bloodstream. Some introverts—like Oishi—may seek protective seclusion in the mountains as a balm against overstimulation; others—like me—may find it in the steady beat of waves or the restful ombré of blue that blurs the line between sky and sea.

When I asked a group of writers what they thought about the connection between personality and landscape, one confirmed introvert said that maybe she liked open spaces because she could "see the people coming." For me, this is certainly true. Before going down to the beach, I often peer down from the bluff to prepare myself for who I might be meeting there.

In fact, some landscape psychologists believe that having a place from which we can survey our surroundings is a critical feature of the appeal of landscape no matter our personality, or whether we prefer mountains, oceans, or somewhere in between. Our hunter-gatherer ancestors may have looked for landscapes that combined overlooks or similar vantage points near areas in which they could take shelter, an idea called "prospect and refuge." And our species may still obtain a sense of security from a landscape that offers both vistas and retreats.

Psychologists are still sifting through ideas about the roots of our attachment to particular landscapes. Does human evolution play a deciding role, or are our childhood experiences more important? In Sweden, researchers found that people preferred the landscapes they grew up in, a finding that was particularly strong among people who lived near the coast. Survey respondents in one study talked about the freedom coming from the coast's open views, the power of the ocean, its appeal to all five senses, and the deep connection we have to water from our own birth.

My own childhood was spent mostly in the chaparral hills of northern California and among the trees and granite of the Sierra Nevada. But when my dad, another introvert, felt like celebrating, he took us to the beach (so perhaps Oishi's research seems to align with my own experience more than I'd thought). But this was not the towel-tiled patchwork of a sunny beach resort, but kelp-draped sand with gray skies and moist air to dampen the sound of the waves and our own voices. Maybe this early memory was enough to give the ocean an enduring power over me.

Sometimes our soulscape grabs us later in life. Geographer Tyra Olstad grew up among the trees and lakes of New York, but when she began doing research in wide-open spaces—deserts, prairies—she found her home. The prairie, Olstad thinks, is not too different from the sea. Standing in the middle of a tall grass prairie, she feels as if she's immersed in water. "You can even feel seasick," she says. Birds startle and swoop out of the grass in flocks, becoming schools of feathered fish against the sky.

Often, psychologists test people's landscape preferences by showing photographs of lush trees, of scenes of saguaro, or vistas of empty waves. It may be no wonder, then, that people in these studies tend to gravitate toward green landscapes. Anecdotally, Olstad says, people who live in the rural Great Plains love open vistas but might not choose a photo of flat fields when asked for their preference because they aren't immersed in the landscape, with the scudding clouds and changing light, the variation by hour and day and season. Photos can't capture the beauty of Olstad's prairie, or of my chameleon sea—the way that time and light flicker through these landscapes, the dependability of the tides, the seasons. They can't encompass how these rhythms pair with the unexpectedness of weather, of motion, of the small chaos of waves that tumble over each other, eager brothers bumping shoulders on the race toward shore.

The rhythmic sound of the waves is thought to calm us; when I wake in the night and I catch that distant rumble through an open window, I turn over and close my eyes. But not everyone is lulled to sleep this way. When I asked Steve White, a long-distance solo sailor who competed in the 2008/2009 Vendée Globe, a round-the-world race, he said something that surprised me. "To be frank," he admitted, "the noise of waves breaking on the beach frightens the bejesus out of me—because if you're on a boat hearing breaking waves, you're doing something wrong."

White's ocean is a different seascape than the one I know. Mine is not the wholecloth of sea, only its frayed hem, seen with my toes safely in the sand or from a few hundred feet offshore. White has sailed across the Atlantic more times than he can count; his ocean is an endless series of grays from sea to sky, with no coastline or other boats to break his view.

At sea, White can be so immersed in meeting the needs of his boat that he doesn't often get a chance to take in his surroundings. But when he does, he takes in a few deep breaths—"just from the bottom of your soul . . . like you've never breathed before." In the open ocean, he's aware of how insignificant he is. "It's humbling and enriching and empowering and many, many feelings at once."

White says life offshore is much easier. "You've got so much space and room." Once he gets toward the coast, that's when he has to be on his game, with boat traffic, reefs and rocks, and the complications that arise from the inter-face between land and sea.

For some, even standing on the shore—feet far from the deck of an oceangoing boat—is too fraught. Jeff Krieger is a New York-based aquatic therapist who runs a program for people struggling with water-related phobias. Some of his clients have never learned how to swim, or had an overzealous instructor who pushed them too much, too soon—but the majority of the people he works with seem to come hard-wired to be afraid of water. They start quaking in water up to their knees, or may go to any lengths to avoid water, skipping family trips, even a honeymoon stroll, hand in hand, down a white-sand beach. It's fascinating, he says, "that we spend nine months in our mother's womb, in water, and some people come out fearful of water."

Now as I stand at the bluffs near my home, I try to imagine what it would be like to be overcome with terror, to see the expansiveness and have it make my throat seize up in fear, rather than in awe. Maybe it's no surprise that water, and the oceans that hold most of it, taps into our deepest, strongest emotions. The ocean can be both a source of life and a place of danger. It's where life came from and where some of us return at life's close. Our prospect and our refuge; our past, our future.

If I wake early and walk along the shore, I'll sometimes see the ocean's edge as a true refuge; the sea caves beneath the bluff often harbor worn sleeping bags in the shadows. For me, the shelter of the ocean is the view itself, the prospect is what it lets me imagine—that I could keep on going, if only I knew how, all the way to the other side.

By-the-Wind Sailor

Come spring, hundreds of castaways wash up on beaches along the central coast of California, blown by the wind. These stranded seafarers, known as by-the-wind sailors, are small enough to fit in my open hand. Their bodies are their craft: each has a flat, oval-shaped float which rides atop the water, translucent and purple-blue as a fresh bruise. When I walk on the beach early in the morning, when the wind and the world are just beginning to wake, the water's edge looks framed in stained glass, shattered and scattered by the incoming waves.

Peering closer at a cobalt float, I see a series of concentric circles that look like tree rings. These are the gas-filled chambers that give these creature-crafts their buoyancy. It takes many sailors to make this ship—the form of this species that arrives on the beach is called a hydroid, a colony of smaller polyps joined together with small tentacles that dangle down into the water, bearing tiny toxic barbs to spear their prey. These barbs are what they share with the other members of their phylum, Cnidaria—a wild-looking, wide-ranging group of relatives that includes sea anemones and the Portuguese man o' war, a species with a toxin that is extremely painful, and occasionally deadly, to humans. While the by-the-wind sailor is sometimes confused with the man o' war, they are a much less dangerous beauty— their toxins are made for snaring only microscopic meals. Still, I leave them be.

There is so much about them that is beautiful. Even their scientific name, *Velella velella*, is a windblown melody. Yet it's their sail, perhaps, that interests me the most. A transparent sheet of chitin set at an angle across the float to catch the wind, the only way they can travel. There is an asymmetry in Velella sails: some have sails that run slightly to the right of the oval float's long axis, while other sails point slightly to the left. Researchers have speculated that the sail's orientation determines where the Velella eventually wash up.

On the outside, I might seem steadier than a by-the-wind sailor, less easily directed east or west by outside forces, more connected to the ground beneath my feet. Yet the wind that brings the Velella here often leaves me disoriented, the gusts green and relentless as if they've saved their energy all winter just for this. My children and I wipe our eyes and huddle inside in the afternoons, away from the beach, while spring-leafed elm branches hit houses in the unsteady rhythm of a faltering heart. My friends say they feel unsettled too, their kids wild and weepy and exhausted. And it's not even fire season yet, when the wind can do more than push us off balance. This wind demands attention—and sharpens my own. When it's here, I notice the slight change in pitch that signifies that its speed is changing, I look up to watch the clouds gallop across the sky. Clouds, like the Velella, with courses charted by the wind.

To a Velella, what we call the sky might be their open ocean. According to Steven Haddock, a Velella expert at the Monterey Bay Aquarium Research Institute, most hydroid colonies attach to the ocean floor and point their tentacles up into the sea. But the Velellas are flipped over, their tentacles hanging downward into the water, only their sail attaching them to the paler blue above.

More than a decade ago, Haddock created a website called JellyWatch, where citizen scientists can report where by-the-wind sailors reach land, and document what direction their sail is set. So far, he hasn't seen a clear indication that the sail asymmetry is what shunts some Velella to the west, and others to the east. The idea of asymmetry affecting direction makes sense on paper, he says, but apparently not in the wild.

Whichever tack it takes, the sail is the only thing that allows many of us to see these sailors at all. Great rafts of Velella float in the open ocean—Haddock thinks there may be many, many more than the hundreds, and sometimes thousands, that wash up on beaches around the world. Despite their numbers, the only time I remember they exist is when the wind brings them ashore. That same wind makes me wonder what else could be out there, and draws me back to the beach to find out. A few days after I see the strandline dotted with sailors, I find what looks like the white feathers of a shuttlecock. I bend to pick it up. Once it's in my hand, I realize it, too, was a sailor, now dried by the sun. My palms do not tingle, but something in me becomes alert, waiting for what else might come in on the wind.

The Sadness of Solving a Mystery

THERE IS A PLACE at the tip of New Zealand's Otago Peninsula where, according to legend, the souls of lost sailors emerge from the shell. These sailors are reborn as albatrosses—downy, big-winged creatures that confer beauty and power on those who wear their feathers. And when the fledglings there on Taiaroa Head grow big enough to launch themselves into the wind over the Pacific, some say the birds bring luck to those who see them as they soar across the open ocean.

When I visited the Royal Albatross Centre there in 2005, I found myself falling under the spell of the young birds as I peered at them from the observatory. They spread their impossibly large wings as if learning to control the strings of marionettes. It seemed nearly impossible that these same wings, in a few short months, would carry them out to sea. The exhibits I saw explained that five years might pass before they returned.

Where these birds went was a mystery. Of all the things I learned about the albatross, this thrilled me the most. I imagined the bird taking its place on one of the early maps or globes that put fairy tale creatures in the spaces where the great unknown began.

Two years after my visit, Bindi Thomas, a specialist in tracking wildlife with satellites, and her colleagues affixed transmitters to the feathers of three of Taiaroa Head's fledglings. A satellite pinged the birds' locations every six hours. The albatrosses first flew along coastal New Zealand, lingering there for several weeks. Then they soared away, eventually zooming toward the coast of Chile, where they foraged until their transmitters went dark. One crossed the Pacific in just 16 days.

Thomas's study should have thrilled me: we now know more than ever about the albatross and its awe-inspiring maiden flight. Instead, I felt strangely disappointed. I'd loved the idea that the albatross had somehow flown beyond our reach for at least a few years. Now, some of the magic surrounding these fledglings had been tarnished.

For me, the ocean has always seemed to be the last true wilderness. But when I first thought about the tracked albatrosses, I worried that with every creature we manage to chart and locate, there would be a little less wonder surrounding the ocean and its vast unknown. I also felt a personal sense of loss: the story I'd told myself about the albatross—the magical spot I'd dreamed up where only the birds could go—didn't exist anymore.

So I decided to go looking for other ocean mysteries— puzzles about where species came from or where they went. Initially, to my frustration, I found only creatures with known whereabouts, questions already paired with answers. But the more I talked with the researchers who had studied the unknowns of our oceans, the more I started to see that every solved mystery contains the seeds of many more to come, particularly when these mysteries are born in the sea.

Take the story of the Atlantic populations of the logger-head sea turtle. For many years, people have kept tabs on the loggerheads' nests on beaches in the southeastern United States. Those who are patient, or lucky, have seen bales of young turtles, each small enough to cradle in your hand, push their way out of their sandy nest and struggle to the sea, often under cover of darkness. These loggerheads would then slip out of sight for a year or more into the ocean wil-derness. Some would reappear on the far side of the Atlan-tic, others near their birth coasts, 10 times bigger than when they left. While scientists later learned that logger-heads' migrations span the ocean, no one knew what hap-pened during their lost years at sea.

Kate Mansfield, a marine scientist and sea turtle biolo-gist at the University of Central Florida in Orlando, wanted to learn more about these young loggerheads' early travels. Between 2009 and 2011, she and her colleagues collected baby loggerheads from their nests, raised them in the lab, then fitted 17 of them with transmitters the size of a pair of dice and released them into the Gulf Stream, about 18 kilometers off the coast. Then they tracked the turtles as they turned north—following what researchers had consid-ered the likeliest path based on ocean currents and observa-tions at sea. The turtles followed different migration routes, both using and leaving ocean currents, and staying clear of cold waters.

Seven of the turtles Mansfield and her team studied ended up in the Sargasso Sea, the clear, deep-blue center of a spiraling ocean current known as the North Atlantic gyre. Mansfield thought loggerheads spent time there at the surface, staying warm atop floating mats of sargassum algae, safely camouflaged from predators while they grow.

Yet Mansfield assured me that there's much more to uncover about the young loggerheads, particularly about the time they spend in the ocean. A lot of the work that's been done so far, she explained, has been based on a limited understanding of how these animals use the ocean. The technology we use to study turtles has funneled us into tracking two-dimensional migration routes from point to point. But turtles, and other species, think and move in three dimensions—and "there's this whole world beneath the [surface of the] ocean," she says, that we're only just beginning to explore.

In fact, for those who love enigmas, the ocean is still one of the best places in the world to look for them. We've only explored five percent or less of the ocean's reaches. And the sea's very nature—its opacity, its depth, its shifting surface— means that no matter how hard we try, says Helen Rozwadowski, a historian of oceanography at the University of Connecticut, Avery Point, "we can't know the ocean in the way we know land." We can only attempt to know it with the tools we have. Our tools today include tiny solar-powered tags and high-flying satellites—and also our imaginations, which create new technology that helps us understand the ocean, and seek out new puzzles to solve. "As long as we keep thinking and imagining," Rozwadowski says, "there will always be more questions to study."

And gathering data with the technology that we dream up can lead directly to protecting the ocean's inhabitants. In the late 1950s, fishermen found large numbers of Atlantic salmon feeding close to the surface off the west coast of Greenland. Soon fishing boats from several nations descended on this region with drift nets. Uncertain where these fish came from and worried about their survival, researchers began studying the fishery. Using tagging data, researchers traced these salmon back to their spawning streams and rivers in North America and Europe. Based on this research, the International Commission for the Northwest Atlantic Fisheries banned salmon fishing in western Greenland's international waters, starting in 1976.

Similarly, future studies on albatross migration may help us figure out how to protect the birds' flight paths. If tagging programs show, for example, that most fledglings spend their growing years in Chilean waters, Thomas says researchers can gather data on how often these birds are accidentally snared by fishermen there and work with them to reduce this by-catch. Learning more about the birds may also help conservationists foresee how the species will fare in years to come. Changes in wind patterns and storms could shift an albatross from its traditional flight path. "When you get an idea of where they go and where they stop," Thomas says, "you can see in the future how they might be affected by climate change."

Understanding where the young albatrosses fly in their first year at sea is just the beginning. One of the tagged birds—named Toroa, a Māori word for albatross—returned to New Zealand in 2014, more than six years after he departed. But his tracking device had stopped recording after 362 days, having likely been shed with his feathers. What we still don't know, Thomas says, is what happened between the time the recording stopped and when Toroa reappeared in the skies above Taiaroa Head.

I've also started thinking about something else that Thomas told me: at one point, Toroa took off down the coast of South America from the spot he'd usually been foraging. A half-day later, the nearby Chaitén volcano began to erupt. Now when I think about ocean mysteries, I think

about Toroa and wonder if he sensed the impending erup-
tion in a way that, for the moment, escapes human imag-
ination. And when next I see an albatross, I'll still feel its
magic, and the good fortune it brings, in the form of mysteries still to solve.

Lonely Abalone

*S*INGLE *W*HITE *A*BALONE: *female, 7, seeks male. Likes: rocky substrate, algae. Looking for a mate who lives within three to five meters. Long-distance just doesn't work for me.*

The white abalone, the first marine invertebrate to make the federal endangered species list, has a problem with distance. In fact, most abalone do. They're broadcast spawners, sending their gametes out into the sea. If a male and female are farther than five meters apart, it's like they're on opposite sides of the ocean—they won't be able to reproduce.

So when something starts to wipe out their population—overfishing, diseases, predators like sea otters—things can go bad, and quickly.

I've always been interested in abalone; I think it's because I associate them with something forbidden. The first shell I saw—at a neighbor's house, when I was young—had same sort of subtle rainbow that come from oily puddles in a rainy parking lot. I thought it was beautiful, but I also thought it wasn't a sort of beauty I was supposed to talk about. (The dark appeal of that particular abalone shell might have been because it was an ashtray.)

I always thought the California coast was the alpha and

omega of abalone. In fact, they're (almost) everywhere: the Atlantic, the Pacific, French Polynesia, New Zealand. In South Africa, they're known as perlemoen; to divers on the British Channel Islands, they're ormers. (In fact, a policeman sporting wetsuit, mask and goggles reportedly made the country's first underwater arrest in 2005 by catching an ormer poacher in the act.)

Daniel Geiger, the co-author of a comprehensive guide to abalone worldwide, said part of the reason abalone caught his interest was because he could travel around the globe to study them. Little is known about their larvae, but it's likely they can't travel too far before finding a place to settle and eat coralline algae. Even then, Geiger said, their lifestyle is cryptic. Juveniles hide in crevices and under sea urchins. Finally, when an abalone nears three or four years old, it anchors itself more visibly to the substrate. It can move, but usually doesn't go far.

As abalone around them disappear, those that remain become increasingly isolated. And apart from in New Zealand, Geiger said, most populations are under siege from a variety of forces, from poaching to disease to the simple fact that often there are too few abalone, too far apart, to reproduce.

Earlier this spring I read about a high school's project to transplant abalone. They're raising green abalone in an Orange County classroom, carefully monitoring the abalone in their tanks, growing as many as 200 to be eventually released into the Pacific. I was excited that high school kids—no matter where they lived—were doing such a cool project. And that there might be a chance of reviving struggling abalone populations.

But Geiger told me transplanting projects have rarely worked. Divers can hand-plant abalones on the rocks—

which means finding a rare spot with no algae or barnacles so that the abalone can get a good grip on the substrate. Or you could grow abalones on rocks in the lab and then transplant the mini-ecosystem—which sounds lovely, but also likely to be costly and challenging.

"It's a real bummer," Geiger said. "The only thing you can do is wait."

Yesterday I watched Neil Gaiman's commencement address to graduates of the University of the Arts in Philadelphia. He talked about the process of so much of his early work as sending messages in bottles—just putting his ideas out there, never knowing what would be read, what might make someone respond.

Abalone seem different to me now. It no longer appeals because it's forbidden fruit, but because it's a creature that's just out there doing what it can. And this makes them more like me and everyone I know. Beneath the ocean, they're casting out their free-floating futures with little hope of response. And I do find myself hoping for them—even more than I hope for myself—that they'll get the answers they need.

Grunion Run

Pᴀᴄɪꜰɪᴄ Bᴇᴀᴄʜ, during a golden spring afternoon, fills with people along the boardwalk and the sand. Older couples walk the community bike path with visors shading their faces while surfers stretch into their wetsuits. A man pushes his bike with an attached green duffel, his middle finger held aloft in front of him like a torch. A woman strolls with a ferret on a leash, a bare-chested young man jokes with his friend in Portuguese. A teenage girl rolls by on a skateboard, licking an ice cream cone. A boy drags ropes of kelp along the beach.

At night, there's a different crowd. At least that's what I hope. I've come here to see grunion—silvery fish the length of a hand that swim onshore to spawn after sunset.

Grunion, found on the Pacific shores of Central and Southern California and Northern Baja, may appear on sandy beaches anytime between February and September. The peak months of April and May are closed to grunion fishing—during the rest of the year, you can catch the fish, but only with your bare hands. Springtime brings not only the grunion's strongest Southern California runs but also volunteers known as Grunion Greeters, who monitor the fish to learn more about them.

Melissa Studer, Grunion Greeters' project director, picks me up from the hotel around 10 p.m. and drives to the far end of the beach that I strolled in the afternoon. She says she often meets people like this—for the first time, late at night, going to see the grunion.

We start at the darker end of the beach. The surfers and strollers have disappeared; the only sounds are those of waves and wind. Studer says that this is one of the draws of grunion greeting—seeing a different side of the beach, one where sand sharks swim into shallow water and shorebirds flicker like ghosts overhead.

The first thing we look for is a "scout," Studer says, a male grunion that comes ashore alone to check out the conditions. Farther down the beach, a few tiny circles of light form constellations in miniature. Maybe they're the flashlights of other volunteers, maybe people out to see grunion on their own.

For many, grunion spotting has the reputation of a snipe hunt—a search for something that doesn't exist. Growing up in Southern California, Cynthia Vasquez thought these springtime runs were too weird to be true, and the few times she did go to the beach to watch grunion, all she saw was sand. "I started to think it was an urban legend," says Vasquez, who is now a volunteer for Grunion Greeters.

Other people have never even heard of grunion. Earlier that afternoon, on my way to Pacific Beach, the cab driver and I started talking about the fish I'd come to see. He asked me to repeat the name several times, then to spell it for him so he'd remember, but I wondered if the word would vanish from his memory as soon as he reset his meter.

The more we talked, though, the more I realized he

was not just trying to make conversation—he was really intrigued. He started to tell me about the turtles he saw as a boy in Africa, where he grew up. Then we talked about turtles in Central America, which always return to the same beach to lay their eggs, then swim thousands of miles in the open sea before they return. The taxi driver explained that scientists are tracking these turtles with satellite tags to learn more about their journeys, and I thought that maybe he'd remember the grunion after all.

Even for those who have seen a grunion run, these fish remain an enigma. Little is known about their three- or four-year lifespan beyond what happens around the beach. Grunion follow each month's highest tides around the times of the new and full moons, catching a ride into shore just after the night's highest tide. The waves wash the fish high on the beach, where the female digs a hole in the sand with her tail to deposit her eggs. As she's digging, a male wraps himself around her and deposits milt that runs down her body and fertilize the eggs.

The eggs, between one and three thousand of them in each deposit, lie in orange clusters under the sand, incubating just a few inches below the surface. The egg sacs are flexible, usually surviving the overhead foot traffic of beach walkers and shell collectors. After about 10 days of incubation, an environmental trigger stimulates hatching—in this case, the next round of high tides, which wash the newly hatched fish out to sea. If the waves don't cooperate, hatching can wait until conditions are right.

Even though the eggs can survive for weeks out of water, they're not invincible. The Grunion Greeters project began out of concern that beach-grooming practices might be harming the species. "The poor little guys, the places that they use for their eggs are public places," says Karen Martin, now a distinguished professor emeritus of biology at Pepperdine University.

Martin, Grunion Greeters' executive director, led the scientific portion of a 2002 pilot program that brought in volunteers to help with the initial count. From there, researchers began working with several organizations—including aquariums, wildlife agencies, and environmental groups—to conduct the first-ever long-term population study of grunion, with the help of an extensive network of volunteers along much of the California coast. Anyone 18 or over can sign up, attend a meeting and learn about the grunion and how to report what they see on the beach.

Instead of individually counting what could be hundreds of wriggling fish, greeters use a measurement called the Walker scale, which focuses on the strength of a run. A W-0 on the Walker scale means a few scouts at most; a W-5 means fish are carpeting the beach so thickly that you can't walk through them without stepping on one. In a W-5, the grunions form "a silver lining along the surf," according to the project's data-collection sheet for volunteers.

During the project's first few years, the reports of volunteer monitors helped determine that "it was pretty clear that grooming over the eggs is a bad thing," Martin says. Since then, many places in Southern California have begun grooming above the intertidal zone, where the grunion lay their eggs. Volunteers also spotted an extension of the run in Tomales Bay, north of San Francisco, that researchers hadn't known about.

In Pacific Beach, we've been out for a half an hour, and the only sign of life we see—other than the flashlights down the beach—is a lone night heron swooping in and coming to stand near the water's edge. Studer tells me that the chances of a grunion run building around your feet are much higher if you're quiet and still.

Then another night heron comes in. Both stand there, looking out at the dark waves. The first fish we see is in the mouth of a night heron, its tail flipping as the bird swallows it.

Scouts come onto the beach, one or two at a time. A man shouts, "They're here!" Then, after a few minutes, more and more fish appear on each incoming wave.

As I watch, the females bury themselves much deeper than I would have thought; sometimes, all I can see is a tiny head swaying back and forth above the sand, looking like a little thumb.

Behind us, the waning moon eases in and out of the clouds. Studer calls this only a moderate run, maybe a strong W-2, as she'll report on the project website tomorrow. By midnight, when we leave, a thin strand of shining fish seems to outline the waves as the fish spread out along the beach.

One night, a few weeks later, I visit the beach near Stearns Wharf with three Grunion Greeters—these ones are graduate students at UCSB's Bren School of Environmental Science and Management who were intrigued by the fish.

The thing that shows up are people. My husband got interested in grunion after hearing about what I saw in Pacific Beach. Then he told a few people in an evening race he was competing in. When we get to the beach at 10:30 p.m., there's a small crowd; as the night goes on without a visit from the grunion, people lie back in the sand and tell bad jokes, making the Wednesday night feel like an impromptu party.

At 11:15 p.m., a single night heron shows up, and I get my hopes up.

If grunion have spawned here recently, their progeny may be swimming in the dark waters just off the beach. Grunion larvae spend about 40 days near the shore, feeding on plankton after they hatch. The juvenile grunion may then travel to harbors or brackish bays. They'll be ready to spawn within a year.

Tonight, no scouts appear. The night heron takes off into the darkness, and soon, the grunion greeters do, too.

Grunion runs have reportedly been a point of gathering for centuries. The Kumeyaay tribe, living in what are now San Diego County and Baja California, feasted on the beach to celebrate the arrival of the grunion. These days, volunteers bring along kids, friends, and visitors when they go out to greet the grunion.

Vasquez found the Grunion Greeters program online and thought it would be a fun thing to do with her five-year-old daughter. They saw their first run together in La Jolla—there were just a handful of the silvery fish, but it was enough to hook them. "Once you see a run, it's addicting," Vasquez says.

In addition to rating the runs, volunteers are gathering information that may be used in the future to monitor beach health. Martin, for instance, has looked into how increased shore or beach salinity—which might occur with the operation of proposed desalinization plants in thirsty Southern California—might affect grunion.

I went to see how the beach scene changed once grunion-hunting season begins. So on the balmy evening before the summer solstice, my husband and I walk with another couple down to a nearby beach and find kids everywhere. The moon, which was full a few nights ago, still hovers large on the horizon, giving off a citrusy glow.

At first, we don't see anything but the wide glade that the

moonlight paints on the water and the lights of the oil derricks in the distance. Then, a night heron swoops in. Soon, a few grunion scouts start to flip their way up onto the beach.

Kids with buckets start screaming. They swarm the water's edge. The run builds quickly, and fish wriggle across our feet as we stand in the wash of the waves. A dog runs through the waves, scooping up fish in its mouth and then dropping them on to the sand.

Cub Scouts catch grunion after grunion in their hands and plunk them into buckets. One of our friends stops a boy from pulling a female out of the sand as she's laying her eggs. The Cub Scouts' leader says they're going to fry the grunion for them to eat.

On the walk home, our first-time grunion spotter friends have already become advocates, talking about how they'll tell their kids about the grunion's beach run. They'll let their kids catch the fish in their hands and then have them release the grunion on an outgoing wave. Years after this night, I'll read a new paper by Martin, Studer, and their colleagues that urges increased protections for the grunion, based on the data that the Grunion Greeters have collected over the years that points to runs getting smaller and smaller, possibly affected by warming waters and an acidifying ocean. They also caution against careless grunion hunting. "All should be able to simply enjoy the amazing sight of California's original surfers dancing on the beach," they conclude.

And there is so much to enjoy. Even now, I remember the cabdriver looking in his rearview mirror and grinning at me after I told him about the grunion at Pacific Beach.

"It's a miracle!" he said to me. I imagine that if I see him again, it will be on a beach. His pants will be rolled up to his calves, he'll be holding a flashlight in one hand. In front of him, wave after wave of fish will flicker in the moonlight.

MARVELOUS CREATURES

Alligator Awesome

THE ALLIGATOR HARVEST at Louisiana's Rockefeller Wildlife Refuge happened every September, so in the fall of 2007, Diane Kelly packed her bags. She wasn't hunting, but she still had to put her scalpels and knife blades and the rest of her dissection kit in her checked bags. Explaining to TSA that she was going to figure out how an alligator penis worked wouldn't fly.

Kelly, a researcher at the University of Massachusetts Amherst, has studied how penises work in everything from rats to turtles, looking mainly at what makes the penis stiff. During graduate school, she scavenged roadkill in Florida to learn more about armadillo penises. Why roadkill? She was a life-long animal lover who was squeamish about sacrificing animals just so she could study them. Then she realized that using animals would be an essential part of her work—and she studied how to do it humanely and to learn the most from each animal as possible.

But still: alligators. She was relieved she didn't have to hunt for them herself. "When they brought them back, they were huge, they were dead and I found them frightening," she says. "If I had gone out myself, I would have been lunch."

Four adult male alligators waited for her when she arrived in Louisiana. One of these was 4.62 meters long. At first, this didn't sound like a very big number to me. But then I realized that if that alligator had visited the swimming pool I went to as a kid, it could have dangled by its tail from the high dive and stretched its body from springboard to surface. Its jaws would be well underwater—it could easily snack on a passing swimmer.

Almost nothing is known about how alligators copulate, since it all happens in the water. But alligator penises had never been seen to change shape or stiffness. In all the other species Kelly had studied—even in the ones that had bacula, or penis bones—inflation was a key part of the penis's ability to get the job done.

Kelly started work at the wildlife refuge's field station first thing in the morning and worked until dinner, with a quick break for lunch. Sometimes it was quiet. Sometimes the radio was on. If it was on, it stayed at whatever station it had been tuned to that morning. She didn't want to get gunk on the dials.

She covered her camera in a plastic bag with only the lens poking out. That way, she didn't have to take off her gloves to change the settings. This was gross anatomy—she would do the detail work later in her lab in Amherst. Gross means big, Kelly says, "but sometimes, gross is gross."

For each alligator, she took the section from the pelvis to the tail and set it up on the table inside the field station.

She took photos before she started. *Click click click.* She removed a layer of alligator. *Click click click.* She took as many photos as she could; she sketched what she saw into her notebook. Working this way, she could study one alligator a day. Sometimes she came back after dinner to finish.

Kelly usually does penile inflation tests on the species she studies. This means she sticks a syringe into the appropriate cavity and fills it with saline. It's something you can only do on fresh tissue—preserved penises can't be inflated, so having the refuge's alligators was a rare chance to see exactly what was going on.

The inflation test had always worked in birds and mammals, and on the outside, an alligator's penis looked something like a mammal's. But when Kelly thumbed down the plunger this time, nothing happened. None of the alligator penises got longer. And they didn't get wider, either.

Later, when she got back to her lab, she'd stain the tissues and see the alligator's penis was just packed with intertwined collagen, with few spaces for blood or lymph to rush in.

At this point, if you were me, you might say something like, "An alligator never has to worry about shrinkage!" But if you're Diane Kelly, you say, "My mind was blown! There was something really different going on here."

But how does an alligator, which keeps its penis tucked inside its cloaca, get this permanently stiff organ within range if it doesn't get bigger? In Louisiana, Kelly tried to find out.

Other animals that keep their penises under cover have muscles attached to the penis that help it pop out of the cloaca. But the alligator doesn't have any muscles that attach directly to its penis. So, Kelly isolated nearby muscles and pulled on each in turn to see what happened.

When Kelly pulled on a muscle within the cloaca itself, the alligator's penis popped out. (One of Kelly's colleagues has a video of this happening spontaneously—he was dissecting a recently-deceased alligator when a metal instrument depolarized the muscle and the penis snapped into view. Kelly says that everyone in the video jumps back.)

At the end of her time in Louisiana, Kelly packed everything up in formaldehyde, loaded her samples into coolers and shipped them back to her lab in Amherst. There, she looked at tissues, she examined the intricate cross-linking of collagen. Her account of the alligator penis appeared in 2013 in the journal *The Anatomical Record*.

Someday, Kelly is going to try to trace the lineage of the penis from the alligators and crocodiles—which she imagines might have a similar system—to the birds. In the meantime, other penises are calling. Monotremes, the egg-laying mammals like platypuses and spiny anteaters, fascinate Kelly. She encouraged me to check out the four-headed penis of the spiny anteater. Only two of the heads ejaculate.

If you're me, when you first see the video, you might say something like, "Ack!" and not be sure whether to be frightened or enthralled. But monotremes' penises may have similarities to two-headed penises of snakes and lizards. And because a spiny anteater, also known as an echidna, also stows its penis inside a cloaca when not in use, it's a bit like a turtle's penis. And an alligator's, too.

If you're Diane Kelly, you say, "It's pretty amazing." And then I remember that Kelly once had to get over a little queasiness, too, so I watch the video of the echidna penis again.

Small

WE CAME BACK from vacation earlier this month to find that someone else had moved in. I didn't realize it at first— the house seemed just as we had left it, and we were busy emptying the car and starting the laundry and repopulating the house with everything we'd taken with us.

It was later, when two of the boys were in the bathtub, that I saw piles of bird poop around the floor in the dining room. The dining room is a small space underneath a green- house window, and it has always attracted birds. I froze, wondering if I'd find a bird huddled in the corner. When I didn't hear anything, I started looking around for a dead bird. I wanted to find it before the kids did. Their toys are in this greenhouse room, too, and I imagined the unhappy surprise of finding a still, small creature when you're reach- ing for a wooden train track.

I crouched down to look closer. And that's when I saw the tiny white ball beneath the table.

I hoped it was a ball. Honestly, it could have been a ball— we'd borrowed a friend's bingo set, and even though we'd given back the cage full of balls, they kept appearing around the house: I-29, B-4. I worked at a summer camp where we played Bingo every Monday night, and I couldn't help coming up with things to say about the number: *I-29, oh how I wish I were 29. B-4, brush your teeth B-4 you go to bed.* This was the same camp we'd just returned from, a place that's layered with memories of my childhood, my college years, and now my sons' childhoods. One of them visited several times before he was even born, when he was the very smallest of growing things.

But the white ball. Seeing it took my breath away because I knew what it was even though I didn't want to. An egg. Of course, it was an egg.

I didn't want to touch it. I am probably not a good candidate for backyard chickens because eggs make me slightly nervous. I worry I will drop them. I wash my hands after cracking them, and if I overcook them and have to scrape them into the trash, I feel awful—wasting an egg seems worse than burning a piece of toast. Each one seems so precious, its own little world.

I also knew I couldn't leave the egg there, where it would get trampled or eaten by our dog. I didn't think it would hatch, but still, the idea of our dog eating it made me really sad, for both the bird and the dog, even though it's likely that neither of them would have thought much of it. And my oldest son, the one who hadn't gotten home yet, would be upset, too; he sometimes worried about eggs and birds in the house the way I did. He was getting a ride home from a neighbor friend, eight hours down from the mountains. Suddenly he seemed very small, hurtling across the state in an oversized pickup truck.

I showed the egg to my husband, who looked around the dining room again. Then he spotted it—a nest that was on top of the mechanism that opens the greenhouse window. Later, he learned from some guys who'd been working in the yard that they'd heard banging and wild chirping inside, and peeled back a window shade to see three birds inside.

He put the egg in the nest and put the nest outside near the greenhouse, tucked on top of a light. It's still there. I haven't looked at it because it makes me sad. Had the bird intended to lay her egg on the ground, or did she somehow miss the nest? Or did know this one would not grow, so hid it away?

From the outside, the egg itself was beautiful, perfect, the largest of pearls. A friend sent me a link to a bird identification website, and it's pretty clear to me that it was a mourning dove: the eggs the same size and shape, the note that the birds are "unbothered by nesting around humans," and that they may nest in eaves, gutters, abandoned equipment.

I'm sure our house did seem abandoned. I have the same kind of sadness around houses standing empty as I did about the egg, sitting on the floor. What use are they, if not filled with life? I know that empty things make space for other things to move in, but it's hard to be in the between time, when something has left but nothing has moved in to take its place.

Then my kids got out of the bath, my husband kindly cleaned up the bird poop, and my oldest son came through the front door. The house seemed full again—fuller, maybe, because something about it had been home, for a short time, to something more than just us.

If You Feed Them, They Will Come

IN 1997, JUST OFF Grand Cayman Island, I stood up to my waist in water so vibrant it looked like it could have dyed Easter eggs a perfect pastel blue. Stingrays swirled gently around my legs. Their wide wings rippled. They skimmed the sand beneath my feet and then kited to the surface. My hands were full of squid, an offering for the rays. There must have been dozens of people around me, but I remember nothing of them, just the soft skin of the rays, and how they nosed into my hands like puppies.

For years, people have been standing in those shallows—a place known as Stingray City—to see southern stingrays, grey or brown creatures with a whitish belly, that feed from open hands. And if the others are anything like me, they're drawn by the promise of an encounter that seems almost like magic—a moment where these wild creatures draw near enough to touch. But in 2001, artist and conservationist Guy Harvey decided to examine how all this attention affected the rays. He and scientists at the Guy Harvey Research Institute at Florida's Nova Southeastern University began counting the numbers of stingrays coming to the site and tagging individual rays to learn more about their behavior and estimate their population size.

We food bearers—about 800,000 of us a year at two different sites—have changed the behavior of the animals. Southern stingrays are usually most active at night, but when researchers tracked the movements of several tourist-fed rays with acoustic tags, they found that the animals swam much more during the day, when the food arrived. Normally solitary, the fed rays crowded around visitors and the food they brought. In these close quarters, the rays became more aggressive among themselves; they suffered more injuries, colliding with boats and with each other.

Some say people's fond memories of the rays at Stingray City help them gain a new appreciation of the marine environment, which may even foster a more profound interest in marine conservation. I know I would like to remember that day just as it was: the clear warm sea, the velvety rays, the way the world tunneled down to what was right in front of me. But if I were to trade out a few things about that morning—switch the stingrays for Dall's sheep, for example, change the beach for a bluebird day in the mountains, fill my hands with carrots—I'd feel very differently about it.

After years of camping, I know that feeding wildlife on land brings no good. I'm used to hanging food in trees or locking it up in bear-proof canisters to keep animals away from a campsite, both for my own protection and for theirs. Free snacks can lure animals toward roads and other populated areas—toward danger. They can come to depend on our food, become nuisances, break things, and hurt themselves and those who feed them.

Regulations and guidelines in the United States and Canada restrict wildlife lovers from feeding or approaching many species of marine mammals; in some areas, these protections extend to other sea creatures as well. But it's not clear how well they're followed. A writer friend in Florida talks about a dock near his house where people regularly feed manatees, despite signs saying that it's both illegal and harmful to manatees. I'd imagine that these people are, just like I am, filled with amazement at what appears from beneath the water, that they're not trying to hurt what they love.

So why did I put aside what I know about feeding animals once I got near the water? As a journalist, I'm used to calling a researcher who's an expert, who has spent years studying exactly what I'm interested in. But there don't seem to be any experts to ask. There are just smart people who have been kind enough to wonder with me.

One of these was the late June Dwyer, a professor emerita of English at New York's Manhattan College, who highlighted the human desire to connect with animals throughout Western literature. When we spoke before her death in 2015, she said that thousands of years ago, people wanted to get closer to animals; in the Old Testament, for example, Isaiah's vision of the glorious future has the wolf living with the lamb, the leopard with the baby goat, all led by a little child.

"We do have this affinity and desire to share space with exotic animals," Dwyer told me, "and marine animals are always exotic." Food is a way to bring them closer.

They're exotic—and yet, for many of us, accessible. To see a wilderness teeming with biodiversity, host to some of the Earth's most fascinating creatures, I don't have to fly halfway around the world. I just walk a few blocks from my home in California to the water to see bobbing kelp and migrating whales. I'm one of multitudes on the planet who live by the water; according to the United Nations Atlas of the Oceans, about 40 percent of the world's population resides 100 kilometers or less from the sea.

Australia's Cockburn Sound, a popular waterway near Perth, is one of these places where people and sea life meet. So I asked Bec Donaldson, a marine biologist who's studied the sound's dolphins, about the special fascination many of us have with marine animals. She cautioned that she had no hard data but she thinks one possible appeal of dolphins and other marine species is that they haven't evolved to fear us. "Many marine mammals may not, at least at first, perceive humans as anything to be scared of."

The highly social dolphins in Cockburn Sound learned by observing other dolphins that they could beg from passing boaters. At first, only one dolphin took fish; 10 years later, a dozen or more would approach boats for handouts. The results could be dangerous, even deadly, with the potential for dolphins to be hit by propellers or tangled in fishing line. Donaldson, who works for Murdoch University near Perth, ran a community awareness campaign to educate boaters and fishermen about the harm in handouts; she gave talks in schools and had signs posted around the harbor. The program met with some resistance. When wild animals are so beguiling, she says, people often lack the willpower to avoid engaging with them even when getting close can harm the very thing they love.

Wallace J. Nichols, a marine biologist and author of the book *Blue Mind*, which looks at the connections between water and well-being, wonders if just being in the water helps people establish a mental state more open to feelings of awe and wonder. The ocean's rhythmic, low-frequency sound, he suggests, may resemble what we once heard in the womb, and it has been shown to help people relax. When immersed in water, the levels of our stress hormones change and reach an equilibrium similar to what's been measured in people who are meditating. And there are generally fewer distractions below the surface than above. As a result, says Nichols, who's spent most of his career studying sea turtles, "when something comes along like a turtle, the focus on it is that much more intense."

In Hawaii, people aren't allowed to feed the state's iconic green sea turtles or other species—but the turtles are quite curious and often engage with snorkelers on their own. Nichols was once swimming above a group of turtles when one rose like a hot air balloon, crashing right into him. That surprise may be the key to our transformative encounters with the wild.

"It all comes down to being truly in the moment, the flow, not knowing what's going to happen, because you're in the company of a wild animal," he says. "They will likely do something that you won't be expecting, and there's something that's very exciting about that because that's often lacking in the rest of our lives."

Once, while surfing, I got caught inside a relentless line of breaking waves. The last wave of the set reared up—much larger than the rest—and I froze. Suddenly two dolphins broke out of the face of the wave and carved arcs along its surface. As I ducked into the dark water, hoping I could hold my breath until the wave passed above me, I remember thinking, *If this is it, at least I'm with the dolphins.*

I don't want to give up my memories surrounding the ocean and its inhabitants, or to stop being shaped by my time in the water. But perhaps when I think of my experience with the stingrays, what I'll remember is that every time I step into the water, I'm not the only creature that is changed.

Snail Season

It is springtime, and the snails are upon us. They are upon the lemon leaves, and the stucco walls, and the umbrella stand. Somehow, they are upon the closet doors, which happen to be inside the house. They are upon the roof rack of the car as it travels six hundred miles north to Mount Shasta, and they emerge unscathed.

Beware to anyone who steps barefoot into the grass at midnight. The walk through the darkened house to the bathroom now seems much preferable to the sickening crunch of a shell beneath the heel.

This is the first place I've lived that had so many snails. During the first few years in this house, I heard an odd sound at night, a cross between a scratch and a squeak. One rainy evening, I looked up. Dozens of snails slid along the greenhouse that shelters our dining room table. (The greenhouse is the addition of the man who lived here previously. I have been to his new house, where he installed an even larger greenhouse room, facing west. Ours, a prototype, is south-facing, and in the winter it is lovely and warm. In the summer, it is hot.) The brown garden snail lays as many as

80 eggs a month, and can breed six times each season. No wonder it feels as if we're being overrun.

We planted three successive patches of sunflowers the summer before last. Each time, the shoots pushed up hopefully through the ground. Then they vanished in a single night. Only when we put a band of copper around them did they grow to tower over the greenhouse, blocking out some of the summer sun.

The copper works, people think, by creating a response in the snail's nervous system that's like an electric shock when the snail's slimy foot crosses its path. But this technique has now reached its limit—it seems unreasonable to fence our yard entirely in copper. So last month, I bought a "natural" snail defense that I sprinkle around the base of the lemon and lime and blood orange trees.

At first I thought this was a deterrent just like the copper. But once I sat down to do some reading, I learned that the iron phosphate I've been shaking on like powdered sugar interferes with the snails' digestion. Their metabolism slows, their bodies slow, and they find a place to die. I shivered.

I am a hypocrite, I know. My go-to method of snail destruction is to send them off to an uncertain end in the green waste bin. They likely feast until the truck from the city arrives, and then, I imagine, they meet the fate that Luke Skywalker and friends narrowly escaped in the Death Star's trash compactor.

I've never tried using two of my favorite things—caffeine and beer—as snail repellent. The caffeine may be toxic to the snail's nervous system; the fermenting sweetness draws the snails in close, and then they drown. I've never tested either of these: perhaps because I don't want to share, perhaps because the effect on snails is too similar to the effect on me.

I could try stopping snails with snails. The decollate snail, with its long, elegant shell, has the good taste to feast on the eggs and young of brown garden snails. Unlike me—even though brown garden snails were introduced to be a food source, and could become high-protein, low-fat escargot, I have no desire to make them part of my garden's bounty. In the citrus-growing county where I live, the decollate snail has been approved for use against other pests. The idea is appealing. The idea of even more snails in my yard, both of which eat lettuce, is not.

In fact, there are so many ways for snails to die that I started feeling a bit sorry for them. In truth, land snails are tiny warriors, nearly every part of their bodies fighting a battle against evaporation. Their shells shield their thin-skinned bodies; their slime attracts water; they can crawl on the edges of their feet to reduce water loss; they can go dormant, or estivate, during heat and drought.

And yet, it had been raining all weekend, and the only afternoon activity that sounded appealing to the resident three-year-old was a snail hunt. We picked them off stucco walls and garden fences, off lemon leaves and lime-colored buckets. We lifted them carefully by the fragile shells. We pulled gently until they released their feet. I pointed out the four tentacles that help snails see and smell.

My son asked if he could look at the foot of the snail, and so we peered closer. The edges of the snail's foot rippled like a ribbon. I thought about how finely balanced snails are, how small in a world of crows and droughts and hands that appear out of nowhere. And then carefully, so carefully, I dropped each one into the green waste bin.

Knight Moves

THE JOKERS in the house are starting to learn the game of kings. The chess set they play with is piecemeal, with a wooden toy horse for a white knight and a lump of rainbow-colored glass for one of the pawns. The board is metal, designed for playing checkers on the road. But still the jokers learn.

Until now, chess has always seemed like a burden, something I should have learned but never really did—like shorthand, or how to fold a fitted sheet. I don't think I enjoyed, let alone finished, the few games of chess I played as a kid.

Yet decades later, I've now checked out a kids' book about chess to find something that makes the game seem less daunting. This is it: there are games that you don't need all the pieces to play.

In one game, The Mad Queen, a line of pawns takes on a single queen. In another, the bishop takes on all the other, stationary pieces in as few moves as possible.

In the process of playing these less-populated versions, we've started talking about our favorite pieces. My sons both like the king. It's true, it's the most valuable. And maybe

I should say the queen is my favorite. After all, when they ask how she moves, I do say, "She gets to do whatever she wants!" with perhaps a little too much glee.

But my favorite—even as a young, apathetic chess player—has always been the knight. It's got a quirky L-shaped movement; it's the only piece that can hop over the heads of the others. (It's also the only movement that the queen can't imitate, although I've read that in some places, once upon a time, the queen could do just that).

It's also the only piece I know how to use better than my sons. They haven't quite caught on to how the knight moves—at least, they haven't yet. I found a list of descriptions of a knight's movement that appeared in chess manuals during the last 100 years or so suggesting that even experts have trouble explaining this succinctly.

Even though it's complicated, it's not new. The knight has moved like this since the earliest days of chess, which some trace to more than a thousand years ago in India. And today, it can play games by itself, too, including a particular one that's been of interest to mathematicians: The Knight's Tour. There are many more elegant explanations of the tour, but here's my low-brow attempt at describing it: you try to move the knight so that it hits each square once, and only once.

Mathematicians and computer scientists are interested in how many possible variations of the knight's tour exist, particularly tours where the knight can return to its original square at the end, called a closed tour. They've found that there are more than 26 trillion ways to go about it on an eight-by-eight square board.

People had also been trying to find ways that a knight's tour can also be a magic square—where all the squares on horizontal, vertical, and diagonal lines add up to the same number. It turns out that you can have a semi-magical square, but not one in which the diagonals also fall into line.

We all have a long way to go before we figure out how to make the knight gallop around the board. But now we've started to try it out around the house, too. We have a battered 60-year-old parquet floor that we've had a love-hate relationship with—until this weekend, when its checkerboard pattern took on new meaning. Last night we played a game of the Mad Queen, in which swiftly, stealthily, each pawn was soon eliminated.

This time, the queen squeezed the pawns and spun them around until they giggled. And then she ordered them to bed. After all, the queen can do whatever she wants.

WEATHER WATCHING

Watching the Weather
in California

At 15, I waited for storms. I wanted drama in my placid life. But when I finally got one—the 1991 Oakland firestorm—it destroyed a few thousand houses, including ours. Afterwards, my dad sank into a depression, my younger brother started climbing out of windows and into trouble, and for years, I felt a lingering instability that took over at unexpected moments on airplanes and ski lifts, even idling at red lights. Even so, a small part of me felt that, at long last, something interesting had happened to me—that now I had a story to tell.

Years later, during the last weeks of pregnancy, I again felt the weight of waiting. Enormous and exhausted, I'd rest my chin on the table during dinner. All my hormone-blurred mind could focus on was the weather.

One sleepless night, I found that the National Weather Service was looking for volunteers to send in eyewitness storm reports. The NWS SKYWARN program started in the 1960s, and now 122 offices around the country have networks of volunteer weather spotters on the lookout for everything from thick fog to thunderstorms. I flipped through a slideshow with photos of tempests overlaid with storm facts, then took an online test. Within 15 minutes, I was a weather spotter. Official papers—a business card, field manuals, a placard for the car in case I had to stop suddenly to observe a tornado—arrived in the mail soon after.

To me, weather spotting sounded like a chance for some badly needed adventure. I imagined the baby and me wrapped in slickers and rainboots, facing down a storm from the seaside bluffs.

I ordered a small weather station. The anemometer went on the peak of the roof, where it could whirl away like the propeller on a boy's cap. The rain gauge sat on top of the carport, tipping out its tiny bucket as raindrops filled it, one-hundredth of an inch at a time.

Before a real storm could come, my son was born. The only memory I have of the weather that day is an overcast haze, where daylight and darkness smeared together until at last he appeared.

I kept waiting. Together, the baby and I sat in the rocking chair, watching the bird feeder and the unchanging blue winter sky. The days and nights were sweet, magical—and still. I was torn between reveling in the quiet and wondering when the adventure would begin.

I woke up one February night when the dog jumped on the bed. Thunder filled the room. I checked the clock: 2 a.m. I was about to turn over when the baby woke, too. I sat up and watched the readout on the weather station while he nursed.

During the next half-hour, it rained .17 inches. Not enough. Then, at 2:32, the cadence quickened. On the roof, the rain gauge's bucket kept bailing, registering nearly a half an inch in 10 minutes, much more than the inch-an-hour minimum required for a report.

I called the NWS hotline, and to my surprise, a real person answered. I gave my report, finding it hard to breathe and talk at the same time. I felt like something exciting was about to happen. When my voice faded, the meteorologist asked, "Anything else?" I felt like I should explain why I was awake—the dog, the thunder, the baby—but I said nothing. "Are you near the Tea Fire?" he asked, talking about a fire that had swept through Santa Barbara's mountains a few months earlier.

I wasn't. I hung up, feeling defeated. If I had only been near the fire, perhaps I could have been more helpful, could have watched for the mudslides he was worried about.

The rest of the winter passed and I had nothing to report. The wind got stronger, but never reached the minimum 25-mph gust. Gentle rain came and went. Eventually, I put the weather station's monitor away.

As winter approached this year, I found the monitor in a closet. This time, instead of plugging it in and sitting, expectantly, in front of it, I called our local NWS district office to find out if it mattered that I watched at all.

Even though our climate is mild, the spotter program's coordinator told me, local spotters have warned of mudslides, inch-and-a-quarter hailstones, even the over-water tornadoes known as waterspouts. And storms don't stay put: Rain in one place can augur snowstorms and icy roads in another.

I should have known this. After all, when I lived hundreds of miles away, in the snow-hungry Sierra, I used to watch for the bright green patches of coastal rain on the TV weather map. But over the years, my life had become more circumscribed. By the time I had my son, the only weather I watched was what was happening outside the window. I didn't think about where it came from, or where it might be going.

Maybe what I was searching for when I became a weather spotter wasn't adventure, but safety. I'm fascinated by the wildness of weather, and yet I want to know what's coming next. But now I know I don't have to face down storms alone. I want to go back and tell the girl I once was that she didn't have to watch out for disaster at every stoplight, that others were checking rain gauges, counting the seconds between the lightning and the thunder that rumbled through her bones.

I want to tell my son, too. Because now he's big enough for rainboots. In one video I have of him, he splashes through a puddle, his face washed with pure delight. When he emerges on the far side, he moves the tips of his fingers together, the sign for more.

What is there to do with a force of nature? Only measure this storm in inches and time, only record what I think I have seen as the weather passes through. My son's fingers meet, over and over. Come on, storms, we're as ready as we'll ever be.

June Gloom

I USED TO THINK the weather was something adults talked about because they were boring. And now that's me, commiserating with neighbors about the state of our sky, which gave us a glorious, bluebird May—and then rolled out a thick cloud carpet on the first day of June.

June Gloom isn't just a Southern California phenomenon, and it doesn't only happen in June. But perhaps we give it a name (and May Gray, and, in dire situations, No-sky July and Fogust) because we complain about it more than people anywhere else.

Sam Iacobellis at Scripps Institution of Oceanography talked me through how Southern California's gloom works. Different parts of the coast offer their own complications, but generally speaking, the cold Pacific water—aided and abetted by the California Current and the upwelling—and a high-pressure region, the Pacific High, conspire to form the marine layer clouds that some of us call gloom.

Usually, the atmosphere gets colder as you head up. But the cold water creates a situation where the air near the water's surface is colder than the air above it: an inversion. The Pacific High pushes air downward, compressing and warming it. Together, this forms a stable inversion that can hold a layer of cloud near the water's surface like an older brother crouching on an upstart sibling.

Gloom often dissipates in the afternoon, as sunshine warms air near the surface. The warmer air mixes into the clouds and starts to break them up.

Of course, there's a lot more than that going on, too. The gloom is the home of a wild kind of cloud field called actinoform clouds, which, to a satellite's eye, look like enormous leaves or pinwheels. And the ocean itself might be providing more than just cold water. Iodide released by kelp may turn into cloud condensation nuclei, which could make clouds thicker and more pervasive.

All this fascinating stuff doesn't prevent me from being boring. But I also think I was a bit too harsh on weather as a conversational topic. Yes, it is something to talk about when there's nothing left to say. Yet it's also a shared experience that has the potential to affect everyone.

When someone I don't know very well says, "This weather is making me crazy," I feel like I really do understand, more than if she talked about how her kids or parents or work was setting her teeth on edge.

Weather connects me to other times, too. I can imagine the Chumash, who were living on this coast long before the rest of us showed up, standing on the bluffs when the clouds start to break up. Those first rays of sunshine feel so needed that it almost feels like my skin is consuming them; I wonder if someone long ago felt this way, too.

Even when the gloom doesn't lift all day, there are ways to enjoy it. There's a contest that's been going on for the last ten years or so among a few Scripps employees to guess the number of gloomy days in May and June.

I asked if there was any trick to forecasting gloom. Events

that affect sea surface temperature, from the El Niño/La Niña cycles to the Pacific Decadal Oscillation—a larger-scale climate cycle—may play a role in the amount of gloom. Iacobellis says the contest is really a crapshoot, but it also has a way of making the gloom seem less gloomy. Each cloud-covered day is one step closer to victory.

And perhaps it's a victory that the fog is still there at all. A number of studies have chronicled the decline of fog along this and other coasts. Rising temperatures are one cause of the vanishing, but there are other factors, too—ocean circulation, the heat given off by urban areas, even the decrease of pollution, which almost always seems like a good thing, but also leaves the air with fewer particles on which fog can form.

Each gloomy day, too, could be a chance to appreciate the gloom while it's here, to remember what's happening out there to make it: cold water, enormous swirls of clouds, that lunk of an inversion layer pinning the gray above our heads. Look out, neighbors, here I come. Now I have even more to talk about.

In Warm Water

Right now, the ocean is glorious. In the evenings, even if the day hasn't been too hot, you can throw yourself into the saltwater and float between the waves for a while without your teeth chattering.

This is not normal. Even in summer (at least for me), any extended taking of the waters requires a wetsuit, if not the full 4 millimeters of ankle-to-wrist neoprene that's needed in winter, and at least some layer of protection. But we've had an unusual warm spell cast over the upper layers of the nearshore waters in the first part of July.

Here's what happened: local winds fizzled, and the upwelling—the cold water that surges up from the ocean's lower reaches, full of nutrients that kickstart phytoplankton blooms and then draw lots of creatures that feed on them—slowed down, shifting warmer water toward the beaches. A fair amount warmer: water temperatures in July were as much as seven degrees Fahrenheit higher than normal.

All this warm water has brought unusual species toward the beaches, especially south of the Golden Gate Bridge. Not just bathers wearing—shockingly—bathing suits, but ocean sunfish, which laze on the ocean's surface to bask. If the warm water sticks around, more temperate species like yellowtail or bluefin tuna could move closer to shore, but cold-water species, including the already-struggling salmon, might suffer.

The waters have also been teeming with by-the-wind sailors (*Velella velella*), jellyfish-like creatures that have been hovering offshore in flotillas so large that some thought there'd been an oil spill. They're now freckling the beaches in August, if freckles could be blue and translucent. It's not quite clear why they've shown up this year in such force.

Some think the warmer water is a sign of a coming El Niño—a strong version of this warm-ocean phenomenon is often linked to more rainfall in California. But the National Weather Services and associated groups just downgraded the likelihood of an El Niño to 65 percent, as the water surface temperatures out farther in the Pacific aren't much different than usual. If one does come, it will probably be weak, and may not make a dent in our drought.

In the morning and in the evening, fishing boats hover several hundred yards off the bluff, their lights trained on the water. They're waiting to net squid, which are running thick and much closer to shore than usual.

I'll be closer to shore than usual, too. I'll float on the surface like a sunfish. I'll hope for rain.

On Tap, Special Reserve

IF YOU WERE a kid in the eighties in California, you might have done things like this: Save the bathwater and flush the toilets with it. Turn off the shower when you soaped up. Heard your parents say, "If it's yellow, let it mellow," and cringe because you knew they were talking about the toilet. You might have even had a Rube Goldberg-like contraption like the one my dad made to use water from the washing machine for the plants. Maybe, like me, you got embarrassed when you saw the signs that read "Save Water. Shower with a friend!" We were all drought experts then. In my freshman dorm, my roommate monitored other people's sinks while they brushed their teeth, turning off the tap with a glare if the water ran too long.

Only then the drought was over. And it's been so easy to forget.

A friend who lives in D.C. asked me what it's like in California right now. And here is the problem—for me, anyway. It's not that different. Turn on the tap and water still comes out. Hot water, cold water, a lot of water, whatever kind of water you want.

Sure, I've noticed things. We went to the Sierra Nevada

in January. The mountains are named for their rugged snowiness. This time, there wasn't any snow, and the mountain lake that we swim in during the summer looked like a lunar landscape. On the way home, crossing through the Central Valley, hills that might be green in winter were the color of an old paper lunch sack. Billboards along farm fences lambasted the politicians thought to be responsible for the water crisis. Closer to home, old ghosts appear as our reservoir dwindles—a WPA-era bridge, the foundations of a long-ago ranch, an island that now is a land bridge to the dry lakebed below.

Still: turn the tap on, water comes out.

Nothing seems to have changed for me, but this isn't the case for everyone. Farmers are steeling themselves to tear out crops and lay off workers. Already-endangered salmon are in a holding pattern in estuaries and river pools. If the river flows are so low that the salmon can't make it upstream, that's another year of salmon gone.

No, the drought hasn't affected me yet. Maybe it won't next winter either. But you never know. During the last drought, the hills got thick with dry brush and grass and leaf litter, and eucalyptus trees stood dead after a winter freeze. A few months before the rains that signaled the end of the drought, a massive fire destroyed more than 3,000 homes and killed 25 people in Berkeley and Oakland.

We stopped saving bathwater after the fire, and the washing machine in our new house was only ever a washing machine. We could only deal with the current crisis: it was too much to think about another one.

But that's exactly what we need to do, said Brian Stranko, the former director of The Nature Conservancy's California Water Program. We've got to get ready for the droughts to come.

Stranko said that one of the state's big hopes is its groundwater. I called him in the first place because I got an email highlighting the connection between groundwater and the drought. And even though a description of the hydrologic cycle somehow made its way into our wedding ceremony—much to the amusement of those assembled—the first thing I thought was: *how does groundwater have anything to do with the drought? It still just needs to rain.*

This is what he said: California's geology means it has enormous reserves—or at least, the potential for reserves—of underground water. We're already tapping into it; in much of the state when we need more water, we dig another well, dig deeper into wells we already have, and pump more water out.

During a regular year, groundwater pumping increases steadily. "During a drought—*Bam!* It's a huge surge," he said. And without other reserves, "you don't have much choice."

TNC and other groups, including several water districts, are working on ways to better manage groundwater in anticipation of future dry spells. One thought is to treat these groundwater sources—the ones that remain, in any case, as some have already been tapped out to the extent that the land has started sinking—like we would a reservoir. We'd figure out what level they needed to stay at to be sustainable; if they started to dip, we'd have to make some tough choices about how to dial back the outflow.

I don't know if this is an answer, of course I don't. I only know how to dip a pail in the bathtub, to let it mellow, to shower with a friend. But it does seem like we need to come up with more reserves, beneath our feet or within ourselves, to deal with this thing that we know is coming, this thing that we still never can quite see before it's here.

Water Year

IT'S OCTOBER, the start of a new water year. A water year, or hydrological year, is one of several ways to measure rainfall. It begins now, the same time we hope the rain will begin, and will end in September. Another measurement, the rainfall year, runs from July to June, creating a buffer of dry season on either side of when the rain might come. Other rainfall tallies use a simple calendar year, from a cross-your-fingers-that-its-rainy January, to summer dryness, then rain again, we hope. We hope.

Different groups use different methods: The National Weather Service in California used to use the rainfall year but switched in 2015 to a water year, following suit with the U.S. Geological Survey and many other water and weather agencies. Hydrologists often like the rainfall year, because streams and rivers can run dry in October. Others prefer the simplicity of measuring the rain that falls during a standard calendar year, beginning in January.

I'm not sure which way I would choose, if I were doing the choosing. A water year gives you the best odds for good early numbers; then you're just watching the clock run down unless there are some late-breaking summer storms.

The rainfall year eases you in with dryness, then it's strong in the middle. The calendar year perhaps is when we need a last-minute miracle. It's probably a good thing I'm not in charge of a water agency, because I'd probably keep changing the system so that the numbers would look good—or at least, not so bad.

I do the same thing with time even when I'm not hoping for rain; I'm always choosing different clocks so that everything turns out the way I want. I don't really make resolutions at New Year's, but I do try to shape the year to come. But if that hasn't gone well, I start again on my birthday, which falls on the spring equinox. Still not happy? I'll try the fall, when school goes back in session, providing another chance to start over, whether or not I'm the one who's getting new pencils and following the bell schedule.

I like the calendars that measure time in other ways. I like the lunar calendar, the shape of the moon from dark to crescent, to half and gibbous, to full and back again. I like the names of the moons that I find in almanacs, where October is the Traveling Moon, the Dry Grass Moon, the Hunter's Moon, the Dying Moon.

I like the names of water measurements, too. There's the word fathom, the six-foot length that describe the depth of ocean and our ability to know or not know what lies beneath. There are the acre-feet of reservoirs, which make me think of a giant stepping through the hills, creating a holding pond for rainfall with each footprint.

Time, too, has its charming increments: the jiffy, the Tatum, the fortnight, the dog-year. There's a song from the musical *Rent* that meters out a year's 525,600 minutes into cups of coffee, bridges burned. Even in the un-measurable units of love.

There was a small storm this weekend, a steady afternoon

rain that brought .41 inches, a daily rainfall record—a good way, I think, to begin our water year. I want to measure this year, and every year, in droplets and inches, rain barrels and gallons. I want to measure it in acre-feet and feet of snow. I will divide it any way I can as if somehow I can make more of what we have too little of: water, and time.

Flaming Pumpkins

MY FATHER WAS afraid of fire. His fear extended to the smallest things: candles, Christmas lights, and even pumpkins.

In 1970, soon after he'd bought a house in the Oakland Hills, a fire destroyed 37 homes. For my father, the threat of another fire was too great to risk for a jack-o'-lantern. On Halloween night, this was his concession—a flashlight inside each pumpkin we'd carved. Christmas was another issue. For years, we put together an artificial tree, decorating it only with ornaments and tinsel. Even holiday lights were too dangerous.

Then, one October, my brother rode his bike to where firefighters watched over the remains of a small brush fire. Suddenly, the winds changed. The firefighters yelled at my brother to get out. For all his caution, my father couldn't stop the flames. That Halloween, 11 days after our house and so many others burned down, I put candles in the pumpkin that I carved at a friend's house while my parents dealt with the insurance company. At Christmas, we got a fir tree that smelled like a real forest. And my father went to a hardware store for twinkling lights that came with fire hazard warnings.

Now it's the season for fires again, and for pumpkins. I get out the LED lights I bought for our pumpkins once I had children of my own. They flicker and dance, almost like flames.

My son is fascinated by emergencies. When he hears sirens, he asks if our house is in danger. I tell him that we no longer live in the fire-prone hills, and besides, it's unlikely that someone's home would burn down twice. But my son is persistent, so I tell him things he can do in a fire: stop, drop, and roll, call 911, stay low to the ground if there's smoke. And then I tell him that this year, we'll turn our pumpkins into real jack-o'-lanterns. Long after he is asleep, I will think of my father as I blow the candles out.

ON THE LAND

Taking the High Road

W E   F I R S T   F O U N D   Yosemite's quiet side in a meadow on our way to Ostrander Hut. After skiing up a wooded slope—the snow-hugging fibers on the bottom of our climbing skins making the uphill easy—we emerged into a snowfield ringed by Jeffrey pines. With only the wind brushing against the pine needles as background noise, we could take in everything: the sharp blue of the sky, the butterscotch smell of the pine bark, and a sunny rock that looked like the perfect spot for lunch. We looked at each other and grinned. Then we shrugged out of our heavy backpacks and started digging through them in search of the jar of peanut butter.

Along with sandwich fixings, our packing list for the nine-mile ski trip to Ostrander Hut, in Yosemite National Park, included telemark skis, climbing skins, and headlamps. Chris and I had avalanche beacons in case the snowpack was unstable, a camping stove and sleeping bags in case we got stuck outside the hut in a nasty storm, a cribbage board in case we got stuck inside the hut in the same foul weather.

The plan, with all this gear, was to spend two nights at the hut, which would give us a full day on each end to ski there and back, and another day to explore the snowy backcountry. We'd both been to the park several times before, but always in the height of summer. Separately, we'd hiked Half Dome, seen Yosemite Falls as it began to ebb in the dry season, and strolled the paths that ran beneath the valley's best-known sights. It may sound brassy, but we felt like we knew the place. Yet every year, we'd flip through the pages of our Ansel Adams calendar and gaze at a different kind of Yosemite, the black-and-white photos of snow-covered pines, of El Capitan with winter clouds behind it—a mysterious place that hinted at a quiet magic.

Conservationist John Muir, who advocated for Yosemite to become a national park gushed over the area's winter charms. "The glorious crystal sediment was everywhere," he wrote after a snowfall in 1871. "From wall to wall of our beautiful temple, from meadow to sky was one finished unit of beauty, one star of equal ray, one glowing sun, weighed in the celestial balances and found perfect." (Muir, who founded the Sierra Club, had much less complimentary things to say about Black people and the Indigenous peoples who first lived in the Sierra Nevada, and the Sierra Club is now working to address this part of its history, as well as racism in the conservation movement that continues today.)

We'd just gotten into backcountry skiing that winter and were looking for a trip to test our ski legs. And so, together, we went in search of Yosemite's winter glories.

The snow gleamed around us after we finished off our sandwiches. Legs already weary from the morning's ski, the sunshine lulled us into a nap as we curled up against our backpacks. After a little rejuvenation, we set off again, following a single pair of ski tracks through the woods.

It could have been the food, the warm day or the lingering drowsiness, but that was about the time our packs started feeling heavy. And we were only about halfway to the hut, with the steepest part of the journey still to come.

Of course, the trek into Ostrander Hut could make any pack seem heavy, no matter what's inside. Getting there takes most people a full day over terrain that gains as much as 2,100 feet in elevation.

On the hut's website, skiers have posted tales of adventure about their trips in and out of the hut. The route is marked with reflective decals and yellow 1937 California license plates nailed high in the trees. But snowstorms and darkness can make the markers tricky to follow. Every day, the hutkeeper radios in to the ranger station at Badger Pass Ski Area, where skiers start their journey, to find out how many people are skiing in to the hut. Once night falls, the hutkeeper may set out with a headlamp to find late arrivals.

Even experts can get turned around. Howard Weamer, the Ostrander Hut's primary winter caretaker since 1974, was on his way into the hut during a storm just before Christmas in 1984. He was carrying a 24-pound frozen turkey and a heavy base radio. "I had absolutely nothing worthwhile," he says.

Along the way, he lost one of his climbing skins and picked up two other groups of skiers who'd gotten turned around. When they got within 200 yards of the hut, Weamer says, they couldn't find the trail markers and realized they had been circling back onto their own tracks. The other skiers decided they'd camp for the night. Weamer gave it one more go and caught a flash of a single trail marker in the light of his headlamp.

"Getting lost," Weamer says, "can happen to anybody." As a result, the hutkeepers recommend that skiers bring in enough gear to spend the night outdoors, in the event that bad weather settles in.

On our way to the hut, however, the skies were the brilliant blue that fills most spring days in the Sierra Nevada. Soon after we set off from the Badger Pass ranger station on a mid-March morning, the sun started to blaze through the trees. We peeled off hats, gloves, and finally, jackets, stuffing everything in the top of our lumbering packs.

The first section of the trip follows the groomed cross-country ski tracks on snow-covered Glacier Point Road. A few miles down the road, two different trails branch off toward the hut. The first option, Bridalveil Creek Trail, turns off from Glacier Point Road after four miles. The second way, Horizon Ridge Trail, turns off the road seven-tenths of a mile later.

Bridalveil Creek is slightly shorter and has less elevation gain; the Horizon Ridge trail has views of Yosemite's peaks and more climbing. The difficulty of each route changes based on snow and weather conditions. "If the weather is good, I would go Bridalveil Creek," says Marcus Libkind, author of *Ski Tours in the Sierra Nevada*, a four-volume series of ski-touring books, and the chairman of the non-profit Snowlands Network. If the powder is deep, he skis Horizon Ridge. "While you climb higher," he says, "the advantage is that you ski on the road that's groomed for longer." Libkind skis out to the hut every year; his most recent trip was with his 13-year-old daughter.

The potential views from Horizon Ridge drew us toward the longer route. An hour after lunch, we started reaping the benefits while climbing the 1,200 vertical feet to the crest of the ridge. Several times, we pulled out the map and compass to figure out what peaks we were seeing. The cluster of three granite domes, including 9,092-foot Mount Starr King, drew our attention first. The sharper peak of Mount Clark, with fingers of snow running down one side, appeared in the distance. And seemingly close at hand, another granite dome that looked familiar but was hard to place among the throngs of white-capped mountains.

We checked the map: Half Dome. It was a view we'd never seen—the rounded shoulders of the dome instead of its sheared face—and, with the two of us all alone on the ridge, it seemed that the view was meant just for us. You might think this ridge would be a good spot to propose.

That's what else I thought might also be coming along in Chris' backpack: an engagement ring. We'd been together for nearly five years and had been talking about getting married for a while. An adventure in the Sierra Nevada, the mountains that we'd spent so much time exploring together, seemed prime for a proposal of sorts.

But when Chris took off his pack at the top of the ridge, what he pulled out instead was his camera. The one he brought was an old point-and-shoot; the digital one, with the self-timer, was inside a jacket back at our house in Truckee. To get shots of us together, we had to be creative. I took a photo of Chris with the mountains in the background; after the shutter clicked, he bent down and drew a line in the snow next to where he stood. Then we switched places. Our plan was to cut and paste the photos together once we got home—a low-tech Photoshop job with scissors and tape.

We spent so long at the top of the hill that, once we finally decided to start skiing again, our packs felt light. But once we skied down into a small saddle and started up the final climb, we realized how far the sun had dropped. By now, six hours into our trip, my legs started rebelling. Halfway up the steepest climb on the route—known as Heart Attack Hill—I was ready to ditch my backpack and everything I'd crammed into it. Chris, who'd hiked the whole 2,650-mile

Pacific Crest Trail and who never seemed winded when we ran, started feeling dizzy.

We stopped and pulled off our packs and spent long minutes eating all of the chocolate chips out of a bag of trail mix. The shadows of the trees on the snow grew longer. We tugged our packs back on and started climbing again.

At last, the trail reached the top of the hill. We kept following the markers through the trees. Just as the pink alpenglow started to fade from the hillside, the glowing windows of the hut appeared, right on the edge of a lake.

Both the rustic hut and the lake, at 8,507 feet, were named for a 19th century sheep rancher who built a cabin nearby. In the summer of 1940, the Civilian Conservation Corps started hauling in materials for the hut along Bridalveil Creek and then up the same hill we climbed with a tractor and an orchard cart. Workers used granite from the glacial moraine, where the hut now sits, for the walls.

From the porch, built from the same granite, skiers can take a few steps down to the lake or gaze up at the rocky buttresses and powder-filled slopes of Horse Ridge. Twenty-five skiers can sleep on the hut's bunks and mattresses, six solar panels run a few light bulbs and the hutkeeper's radio, and the 125-gallon water tank that feeds the kitchen is filled with lake water.

We had stayed at several huts on hiking trips, and even at a few ski-in yurts, so we thought we were professional hutgoers. But when we opened the front door to see the feast that another group of skiers has set out on the long tables inside—bottles of wine, plates of steaming food—we realized that when it came to the Ostrander Hut, we had a lot to learn. After unrolling our sleeping bags on a pair of mattresses in the hut's second story, we boiled water for our pre-packaged backpacking meal in the small kitchen and watched the others eat. We were already planning another trip and the delicacies we'd bring next time.

The Ostrander Hut seems to do just this—lure people back year after year, or even more permanently. Weamer, the longtime hutkeeper, came to the Yosemite Valley in the early 1970s to work on a doctorate in geology and aesthetics, studying how 19th century tourists described their first views of park. During his first winter at the hut, he packed in a 10-volume set of John Muir's works and set up an old door in front of a north-facing window to use as a desk. But somehow, the hut took over; Weamer didn't finish the dissertation, but he's skied and taken photographs all over the Sierra and written a book about the hut and its history, *The Perfect Art: The Ostrander Hut and Ski Touring in Yosemite.*

It's easy to see the appeal. The place has the feeling of a scaled-down sleepaway camp. There are plenty of activities: skiing, strolling, and even skating—the hutkeeper keeps a dozen pairs of ice skates on hand for when the lake freezes over. At night, skiers play cards, read, or stretch out on the bunks while the stove hums away. Outside the hut, a star-packed sky dazzles: it takes a moment to reorient to familiar constellations—the Big Dipper, Orion—when they're surrounded by the hundreds of other stars visible on a dark mountain night.

Even though the hut seems far removed from the rest of the park, let alone the world, this quiet existence is often under threat. Weamer says he's "always a little bit nervous" about Ostrander's long-term survival. At the moment, the person in the park superintendent's seat is an avid skier and hut supporter, Weamer says, but "it takes people of goodwill in the right places, and there's no guarantee that will always be the case."

When we woke up the following day, the other skiers

were on their way out the door in hopes of getting a long day in the backcountry. They had many options, from doing laps on the 600 vertical feet beneath Horse Ridge to a day trip out to Buena Vista Peak.

After an hour enjoying our oatmeal and the hut, silent except for the stove working away, we climbed a mellow slope on the east end of the lake. We pulled off the skins and linked curving turns down into the trees below. Several runs like this and we retreated into the hut for peanut butter and honey sandwiches and another stint by the fire.

In the afternoon, the sky turned a steely gray. News of an incoming storm crackled over the hutkeeper's radio. We wanted to get outside one more time. Even though the snow showed no sign of moving, we pulled out our avalanche beacons to practice with, so we'd react quickly if one of us ever did get caught in a slide. I buried mine and Chris found it within a few moments. I had more trouble with the search; I circled and circled around the spot where he had hidden his beacon for long minutes before I pulled it out of the snow.

Just to make sure we didn't carry our shovels in for nothing, too, we used them to build a ski jump on one of the hillsides, then took turns going off it. Chris snapped a few photos of me from the ground level to make my airborne inches look more death-defying. When I hiked back up to the jump, Chris dropped down on a bent knee and rooted around in his backpack.

"What?" he asked, seeing me watching. He snapped down the cable bindings onto his boots and stood up again.

In the hut that night, rumors about the storm circled around the bunks. The next morning, we woke up early so that we'd have enough time to ski out if the storm hit. Another group had taken off before dawn to beat the weather; at 7 a.m., when we left, the sky was clear, but the snow was hard and shiny with ice.

Scared of skidding and being dragged down by my heavy pack, I eased down through the trees, trying to find rare patches of softer snow.

By lunchtime we were out on Glacier Point Road. I hadn't taken any falls, but every time I sunk into a turn, my boot bit into my big toe. Once we got back to the car, just after two, I pulled off my boots and slipped into my clogs with relief. With my feet propped up on the dashboard, I looked up at the slopes of Badger Pass and the clusters of skiers gathered on the hill. We'd gotten away from this and found the Yosemite of Ansel Adams' photos after all.

The storm we worried about never materialized. Before we left the park, we took a walk on the path to Yosemite Falls. The sun was streaming over the valley's granite walls and the pathways leading to the base of the falls were nearly empty. We took more photos with the ancient camera. First, I stood in front of the falls. Then I dropped a pine needle into an X next to where I stood. Chris stepped in, and I took a photo of him in front of the white mist.

We still have the photo of the two of us in front of Yosemite Falls. A piece of tape holds the two halves of the photo together, and our shoulders almost line up. The falls appears as a single band of rushing water. It's no Ansel Adams, but I like it anyway.

On my next trip into the Ostrander Hut, I'll have a better idea of what to pack. I'll be sure to put in a digital camera and a bottle of wine—and ditch the badly fitting boots. And I'll always make room for an avalanche beacon, no matter what the snow's like. You see, the next December we took the beacons out on another snowy hike to practice. It still took me too long to find the one Chris had buried, but when I dug it up, I found a handmade ring box attached by a piece of string.

Depth Afield

I HAVE A COMPLICATED relationship with photography. Once, on a hike with my boyfriend up Spencer Butte in Oregon, he paused to take in how the sun—something we hadn't seen in weeks—poured through the Douglas fir and splashed against the ferns. "Look," he said, "it's just like a photo."

Maybe it was early, or maybe I was just more prickly than usual. "It doesn't look like a photo," I remember snapping. "It just looks like itself." We didn't talk again until we'd reached the top of the butte.

Later, I apologized. And then I wondered why I'd spoken as if photos didn't matter. After all, I was the one who'd spent nights in a darkroom in college, trying to unveil stark, sublime landscapes on paper the way my favorite photographers did.

My camera was enormous, with a clunky body and a penchant for eating the film I unrolled inside it. Still, I hauled it from California to Alaska, from the Cascade Range to the Sangre de Cristo Mountains. I finally abandoned it in a Santa Fe pawnshop, feeling as if it held secrets I would never know. Perhaps when I snarled at my boyfriend, I just meant that the light through the trees was something I could never capture on film. I thought so much about whether I'd be able to reproduce a particular scene that I barely experienced the moment unfolding in front of my lens.

I started putting other people's photos on the wall. I bought prints of the ocean when we lived in the mountains; prints of the peaks when we lived by the sea. After we got married, we hung a 1913 photograph of a lake where we'd both lived—a wedding gift from friends who knew we were trying to create our own history there—in the bedroom of each house we moved through.

And every year, I still buy the same calendar: an Ansel Adams with an enormous single print poised above each empty month. I always look at others in the bookstore, but this one ends up on the kitchen wall.

So I asked Martha Sandweiss, a Princeton University historian and author of *Print the Legend: Photography and the American West*, why people are so attracted to Western photographs—hoping, really, that I'd learn something more about myself.

Photography, she said, became a way of reframing the country after the Civil War. "The West was a place beyond history, during a time when recent history was really painful," Sandweiss said. Many landscape photographers kept their cameras trained on the wilderness and its prospects, often omitting the West's history and people to create a powerful illusion of a place where only the future mattered. "There's this intense desire to imagine the West as our last great hope."

I wonder if that's what I'm after as I buy these calendars: a place of hope. Each new year spreads out beneath images that show only beauty. My own photographs were never like this—they were always a little out of focus, or holding strange shadows, never quite capturing the awe I felt as I looked at that lake, that mountain, that stream of light. I need someone else's vision to remind me of what I saw, just as the clean calendar reminds me of someone else's life. Something less messy, more perfect.

My calendar stays empty only until I get home from the bookstore. Even months in advance of the coming year, there are already deadlines, birthdays, appointments and play dates that need to be remembered.

These days, I'm spending even more time looking at photographs. Not yet 2, my son can already slide his finger across my phone's screen to see images of his grandmothers, his friends, himself. These people are his landscape now—their faces his Half Dome, their hands his bare tree branches. The photos don't show everything. They don't show late nights or bathroom cleanups, not discontent or frustration or anger. I wonder how he will see them someday. Perhaps as a time less complicated, a place of hope.

He notices more than I realize, even now. The other day, I peeled up the pages of the calendar as I tried to scrawl in another meeting. "Moon," I heard him say.

"Can you see the moon?" I asked as I wrote. "It's not dark yet. Maybe we'll see it tonight."

As I flipped down the page, I glanced up to the print. There it was in the picture, a speck above Adams' dark California valley: Moon.

When I turned, he smiled and pointed, as he must have been doing all along. Maybe that's what photographs are for—to teach me to recognize the beauty that is already in front of me, if only I would look.

One afternoon not long ago, our family made its way down wooden stairs to a nearby beach. The fog that smothered the coast for weeks had lifted to reveal an expanse of water freckled by kelp, sailboats, and the Channel Islands in the distance. "Isn't that just a picture?" my husband said.

This time, I kept my mouth shut. We were loaded with shovels and towels, sunscreen and surfboards, but I stopped for a moment and tried to see like a photographer. Or like my son. Whether or not I can preserve the moment on film, I can at least try to truly see it: I'm in the lens, and the lens is in me.

Landscape Poetry

SINCE CHILDHOOD, Tom Killion has considered the
poppy-strewn slopes of Tennessee Valley his playground. He
and his brother, who were raised in a small town north of
San Francisco, would play Revolutionary War on the gentle trail leading to the pebbled beach, dubbing a pile of dirt
on the former ranchlands "Bunker Hill." Later, they would
scatter their father's ashes here in the valley.

In the spring of 2011, Killion returned again to the valley—part of Northern California's Golden Gate National
Recreation Area—and began work on a new print. He
quickly drew the pocket beach, cliffs, and the sea, scribbling
in the colors and details he wanted to include. He envisioned
a bright, Southwestern light in the sky, the clouds rippling
and catching the sunset.

But after going through the exacting, 250-hour process
of creating the print—which involves transferring the sketch
to a key block, carving that block and others to add layers
of color, then using a small hand-cranked press to print the
image on fine Japanese paper—he wasn't happy. The yellow was too bright. "I almost threw all that paper away and
started over," he said.

Instead, he kept tinkering using a host of tricks he'd learned in more than four decades of printmaking. He carved more details into his color blocks, inserted bits of wood between the press and the paper to make certain colors pop, and added layers of color. Eventually, the print "took on its own life."

"When things start going in a certain direction that I hadn't really planned, I just go with them," Killion said one morning in his studio, which sits a few paces from his house and overlooks Tomales Bay in Point Reyes National Seashore. He pointed out the purples, grays, and pinks that backlight the beach, and the sunset light, stippled with golds and greens.

Tennessee Cove and dozens of other seascapes appear in Killion's most recent book, *California's Wild Edge: The Coast in Prints, Poetry, and History*. The book brings together Killion's wood- and linoleum-block prints, his writings on the cultural history of the coast, and the work of California writers, including Pulitzer prize-winning poet Gary Snyder, who collaborated with Killion on the project.

The printmaker and poet first met in the 1970s. Snyder was a hero to Killion, who attended a memorable 1972 reading at University of California, Santa Cruz, which ended with a giant clap of thunder and a power outage. In 1975, Killion took one of the 100 hand-printed editions of his first book to Snyder's home in the Sierra foothills.

Twenty years later, the pair began their first significant collaboration, a handmade book about the High Sierra. At first sight, the Sierra prints "stole my heart," Snyder wrote. "He had caught the streams and mountains as they are: visionary and earthy; icy, aloof, and dangerous; but an inspiring teacher when approached the right way."

I'd had my heart stolen by Killion's Sierra prints, too.

When I first saw them at an art fair in Santa Cruz, I made a mental note—someday, when I was no longer a graduate student, I would buy one of his prints. Every few years, I'd look through his prints online and wonder how I'd chose, each image of peaks and alpine lakes better than the last. Then, one day, I came across a view that made me feel almost dizzy. It wasn't of the Sierra at all, but of a ridge on the east side of San Francisco Bay, the same ridge that I once saw through the windows of my childhood home.

I'd loved this ridge so much that I'd given names to the patterns of chapparal and grassland that covered its hills. But when I saw Killion's print, it was the first time I'd seen the ridge in years—after our house burned down, we didn't return to the neighborhood. Seeing the ridge again, through Killion's eyes, brought back the sweetness of that early love of the land.

Killion's own love for the land fuels his work. For Killion, the force behind his landscape art is topophilia—an intense love of place. "I am very visual, and my favorite form of beauty, other than human, is the landscape of western North America, with its wide spaces, open grasslands, and mixed forests," he said.

His interest in art was sparked at a young age, when his mother took him to an East Asian art exhibit at San Francisco's de Young Museum. He recalls being fascinated with the mountains and rivers he saw on the scrolls, which reminded him of his own world on the side of Mount Tamalpais, the 2,571-foot peak across the Golden Gate from San Francisco. Soon after, his parents gave him a book of prints by Hokusai, the Japanese printmaker best known for his series of images of Mount Fuji. "I thought, 'Wow, I want to make art that looks like that, in my landscape,'" Killion said.

He began making prints in high school; in college, he

took letterpress printing classes and produced his first book, a compilation of Hokusai-inspired images of Mount Tam, as locals call it.

After graduation, Killion traveled throughout Europe and Africa, and then attended Stanford University, where he completed a doctorate in African history. He later taught African history at Bowdoin College in Maine, and studied in Eritrea as a Fulbright scholar. Over time, however, he started to wonder why he was so focused on a place not his own. "California really is my homeland, of many generations," he said. In 1995, he returned to teach African and California history at San Francisco State University.

All along, Killion had been creating limited-edition books of his prints, which captured scenes from his adventures in California and abroad. When Malcolm Margolin, the founder of Heyday Books, first encountered Killion's hand-printed *High Sierra* book in 2000, he was smitten. "It was the most beautiful thing I'd ever seen." he said.

Margolin went on to publish *The High Sierra of California*, the collaboration with Snyder, which includes Killion's interpretation of iconic Yosemite scenery, the wilderness backcountry of Sequoia and Kings Canyon National Parks, and the region's junipers, streams, and granite peaks. "I just love the forms in the Sierras," Killion said. "Each tree and plant and even the rocks—they all have this individuality because it's such a harsh landscape and you don't have a whole big forest in a lot of places." Running alongside the images are excerpts from Snyder's backpacking journals and writings by naturalist John Muir.

The book raised Killion's profile, allowing him to retire from teaching to focus on his art. He and Snyder followed up with a book about Mount Tam and the 2015 collaboration about the coast. With each project, Killion has immersed himself more deeply in writing about the region's history; *California's Wild Edge* includes chapters on early exploration by the Spanish turn-of-the-century horseback travelers and poet Robinson Jeffers. "I finally found a way to put history and printmaking together," Killion said.

For more than three decades, Santa Cruz was Killion's home base, but in 2003, he returned to Marin County with his wife and two children. His newfound proximity to stretches of undeveloped coastland led to a series of artworks; when he learned that Snyder had also been influenced by the time he spent on this part of the coast, the book took shape. Snyder, a former merchant marine, encouraged Killion to think of the coast as seen from the sea—which led Killion to go deep into seafaring literature, such as Richard Henry Dana's *Two Years Before the Mast*, which describes California through a watery lens.

Snyder also inspired one of Killion's best-known prints. In 2007, the two went on a trip for writers and artists into Sequoia National Park's Miter Basin. One day, Snyder and Killion hiked to Siberian Outpost, a barren stretch of land dotted with rocks and pines. On their way back, they noticed two lodgepole pines growing side by side, their roots intertwined. Snyder told Killion about a Japanese Noh play in which a devoted older couple becomes a pair of pine trees. Killion later headed back to the spot with a camp chair to sketch the intricacies of the foliage.

In his small shingled studio—crowded with printing blocks, sketches for future projects, a small press, worktables, and carving tools—Killion quickly found the lodgepole print and pulled it out. The golden sheen of the trunks comes from the resinous pitch that the high-elevation trees produce to protect themselves. In the summer "they glow, especially at sunset," he said. "Just like candles." The print will likely become part of Killion's current project, a book on California treescapes.

Most of the book will feature new prints, which will take him back into the mountains and along the coast to sketch. In an artist's statement, he wrote about his "love for the natural world, the bones of the land, the skin and fur of the plants and trees." This wild creature is his first and deepest love. "That's why I make my art," he said. "It's the beauty of the real world that I'm entranced with."

Both those things—the tangible wilderness and representations of it—are critically important, in Margolin's view. He recalled a talk and slideshow Killion gave at Yosemite's Ahwahnee Hotel. When the printmaker came to an image of Half Dome, he stopped. "This is ridiculous," he said. "I'm showing you an image of Half Dome, and it's right out there."

Yet in the moments when these landscapes are out of reach, Killion's prints help us recall the places that we love. His work has given me my childhood hills back; they now hang above my couch, a slightly different view now, but with even more layers of love. And art is not ridiculous or redundant, Margolin said. "Beauty leads us to knowledge and understanding and to a relationship with the world. If anything is going to save us, it's not science. It's beauty, it's art," he said.

Rainbow Connection

THE OTHER DAY, as our kids played around a big, messy tree, a friend told me she was going to show me a picture of a eucalyptus she knew I would love.

A eucalyptus? Not one of these troublesome trees, I thought. But then she held up her phone. I peered in at the photos, and then we grinned at each other. I did love it.

The photos were of a rainbow eucalyptus, which has bark that looks like it's been painted with every one of our kids' favorite colors. The bark peels off in strips, and what's left behind is chartreuse and purple, orange and amazing. According to one botanist, the tree's thin, transparent layers of bark reveal the underlying chlorophyll and tannins, and how levels of each change over time as many layers of bark peel away. This species, *Eucalyptus deglupta*, grows in island forests of the Philippines and Indonesia.

The eucalyptus trees we have here have peeling bark, too, and they're also from across the Pacific, but rainbows don't beam out of their trunks. They're actually a pretty sore subject in California. These trees, mostly blue gum, were brought in first to beautify the Golden State—less gold, more green—and then as a potential wood product. They're called gasoline trees in Australia, they're called invasive species here—and yet they're one of the state's icons, and people tend to feel very strongly about them.

I'm not a eucalyptus hater, but I've always been skeptical, I guess, mainly for personal reasons. There was a grove of them behind the biosciences building at UC Berkeley that was both creepy at night and the site of multiple assaults. Many blame part of the rapid spread of the Oakland Hills fire on frost-burned eucalyptus—their oils, their leaf litter and shards of bark.

Even so, by evening I was dreaming of planting my own neighborhood eucalyptus invasion. Rainbow trees, they could do anything! If people saw these trees, wars would stop, credit card companies would stop charging interest, and we'd all break out into song, right?

Unfortunately, these trees are extremely water-loving and extremely tall—liable to get whipped around in strong Santa Ana winds. Planting a 200-foot tree next to our 15-foot roof during a drought would be plain foolhardy.

So we are resigned to the trees we have. But there are things about them that can delight, too. As winter comes on, thousands of monarchs will cluster like grapes on the eucalyptus in a nearby grove. The butterflies can be hard to see, looking like so many dead leaves in the dim light beneath the canopy. But when the sun pushes its way through, the butterflies rise from their perches and swirl like orange confetti among the trees.

Even at the park the other day, all the kids took pieces of the peeling bark and sliced them through the air like cutlasses before racing back to their pirate ship. Later, I found the small seed pods that mark the eucalyptus stuck in the pockets of two different pairs of pants.

I held one in my hand for a while and looked at it. I'd

collected these pods once, too. There's always a marking on one end—sometimes it's a star, other times it's a Y-shaped slit. This one had a small cross. Long after the pants were clean, the pod sat next to the dryer, a treasure of uncertain value that I couldn't make myself throw away.

Can 58,800+ Small Lights Help Us See What's Right in Front of Us?

AFTER MONTHS OF being at home, this winter I went a few hours north to Paso Robles, a place where the rolling hills gathered together. The landscape felt stricken: the grass brittle with months of California drought, the dirt cracking. The people around me seemed battered, too, uncomfortable in heavy coats, eyes tired above their masks. We plodded along on paths through to a valley that was pincushioned with what I knew were lights, but looked like small bubbles on stems. We tried to perch on railings and were told not to sit on the railings. We shifted over, we made space, we wondered how long this would take and how much colder it would get.

Then the lights turned on.

It was a subtle thing: at first just a small brightness, then a steadier glow. I wasn't sure whether to look at a single light and watch it cycle through a rainbow of colors, or to expand my view so I could see patchworks of color emerging in waves across hillsides, into small valleys, rippling around a coast live oak. White and blue, purple and orange, each getting more intense as the sun continued to set, and then vanished. The air grew colder, but something else felt more alive: people seemed to crackle with quiet energy, to pause, to help search for a misplaced set of keys, to make an extra space on the hay bale. The 15-acre light installation by British artist Bruce Munro seemed to spark something new—a communal energy that somehow used the technological wonder of the artwork to enhance the natural beauty of the surroundings, from the oaks that seemed to grow up through the lights to the silhouettes of our own species in the growing dark.

All year, I'd been lamenting the technology we needed to get through the pandemic: the endless Zooms, the online classrooms, the sites where you could play board games at a distance, the telehealth appointments. All things that I was grateful for—they kept me healthy, sane, made me temporarily feel less alone. But like so many other people, I had trouble returning into my body and the world around me after so much time spent receiving and giving information and energy through a screen. The world often felt both out of reach and unreal once I tried to return to it. But here, fiber optics and projectors and solar power made the landscape more, not less, beautiful.

It's not that I wasn't aware of the technology; before the sky went fully dark, the small white lines of electrical cords were visible as they coiled on the surface of the field. But being among all of these small lights brought me closer to the landscape, and to myself, in a way that the faster, "smarter" devices that I'd relied on couldn't. These weren't spotlights that forced the landscape to display itself. The illumination almost seemed to come from the air around me, or from within the land itself. It was an imagined thing, but still: there I was, breathing deeply in the crowded dark, as if the light itself could find its way into my lungs.

Something about this glowing field reminded me of a conversation I had a few years before with Troy Magney, a biologist, as he was moving from Los Angeles to a new job in Davis. It was nighttime, and he was driving along California's main north-south artery, Interstate 5, the hills of Paso Robles a few dozen miles to the west. In the dark, the hills would have been almost invisible, the road lit instead by the oncoming lights of the big rigs heading south, the red tail lights to the north. We'd talk for a while and then the line would go dark, too, for a moment, as he passed in and out of range.

Magney studies light of a different sort: the kind given off by the work of photosynthesis, when a plant or tree turns sunlight, carbon dioxide, and water into energy. Chlorophyll is what makes plants green. It also collects energy from the sun, and when this happens, one of its electrons is bumped into a higher energy state. When the chlorophyll settles down again, it releases a photon, a tiny packet of light.

A tool called a spectrometer can capture this unseen light, and Magney has used them in several western forests. Spectrometers can see the fine details of how a tree's photosynthesis changes with the position of the Sun in the sky or the brief transit of a cloud. The dramatic change is seasonal: although evergreen trees don't look much different to us in the summer or winter—that's how they got their name, after all—they go nearly dormant when it comes to making energy so that they can protect themselves from harsh winters.

Their light, seen by spectrometer, begins to shine again come springtime. And once they start taking in sunlight to transform, it's full-throttle, Magney says. "They go from zero to full photosynthesis within a week or two."

Magney and his colleagues think this is important because

they want to be able to track photosynthesis around the world, as the turning wheel of sunlight to plant energy is also what pulls carbon dioxide out of the air. To measure global CO_2 levels, they want to see how large forests are working as carbon sinks, year after year. Looking at this light that trees produce, Magney says, "could give us a pulse on the biosphere." The light signals sent off by trees can tell us more about their health, too. Stress from beetle infestation, or drought, almost immediately tamps down the rate of photosynthesis—so a dimming of their light could provide an almost immediate indication that something's wrong.

The idea of trees' invisible glow has stayed with me through the years, as Magney has expanded his work to other forests, to newer, more sensitive equipment that can see trees in a way we can't. It makes me wonder what else is out there, glowing, without anyone to notice. Not that it needs us to notice. Evergreens will keep gathering sunlight whether or not we are watching. But something that reveals more connections—between the trees and the sunlight and the air we breathe—seems to fill some sort of lack.

At a 2014 conference at UC Santa Cruz, Ursula K. Le Guin gave a talk that, in part, discussed moving beyond considering the world as disposable and seeing technology as the way to fix it. "To use the world well, we need to relearn our being in it," she said—not only in terms of returning to our kinship with other animals, but to other living and nonliving beings. Plants. The landscape around us. She described this relationship as complex and reciprocal, with humans "as particularly lively, intense, aware nodes of relation in an infinite network of connections . . . infinite but locally fragile, with and among everything—all beings— including what we generally class as things, objects." At its best, could technology help us envision the connections that we cannot see, or even imagine the connections that we have yet to discover?

For Munro, bringing new connections to light took both immersion in the landscape and time. After living in Australia for eight years, he and his future wife planned a farewell tour of the country before returning to the UK. Munro had heard about Australia's Northern Territory, its red desert, the iconic rock formation of Uluru, but he didn't expect much. "I was quite cynical about it," he says now. But when he visited the desert and the rock monolith that has been a sacred, living landscape to the Anangu people for tens of thousands of years, something changed. Munro remembers energy, electricity, feeling fully alive. "The whole desert has this presence that's in the air," he says.

He sketched and wrote about the experience for years before starting to experiment with fiber optics in the field outside of his home in Wiltshire, in southwest England. Acrylic stems, topped with glass bulbs, would be like seeds scattered in the desert—dormant, then bursting to life when conditions are right. Since then, he's brought these lights into new landscapes. In Paso Robles, where I saw Munro's Field of Light at Sensorio installation, there are more than 58,800 of these small seeds sown in the hills, powered by the Sun—and as it sets, the seeds come softly into bloom. Munro and his team of collaborators, from electricians to installers, have tested the LED projectors they use to keep the light at low levels, gentle as starlight, to draw viewers' attention to the landscape instead of outshining it. At another of Munro's fields of light, this one in Uluru, having the Milky Way overhead makes the experience feel "as if you're standing in a ring of light," he says.

The stars above Paso Robles were not as visible. Still, after an hour of wandering through the fields here, I could see more beauty in the barren hills, and in the crowd of people who, in the midst of a pandemic winter, seemed to be lit from within.

When a too-bright light flashes across our field of vision, sometimes the afterimage of the light remains even after we look away. The way this happens is not well understood, but it may be something called retinal inertia, where the cells at the back of the eye continue to respond to the light even after it is gone. I understand even less about what has lingered after being in these fields of light.

It's true that even now, if I close my eyes, I can remember the color that unfurled itself across the darkened field, the way these small lights drew attention not just to themselves, but to the oak trees, the hillsides, the dark sky. But there's another afterimage that still seems imprinted on the space between the shoulder blades, the back of my lungs, the far side of my heart—the places in my body that keep reminding me that among the lights, people were good, and the world was more beautiful than I understood. An afterimage that, I hope, will not fade.

Off the Map

Starting Odometer Reading: 60937

The maps we take to Baja are a community effort. Friends have scribbled on them in red crayon, purple pencil, black ink. *Don't camp here*, one note reads. *Fish tacos*, reads an arrow pointing from the town of El Rosario. Elsewhere: *West-northwest swell. Windy. Maybe gas.*

On that map, on all maps, the Baja peninsula dangles below California, an 806-mile carrot for surfers, kayakers, wildlife watchers. Imagine a scene from the movies, where the heroes' journey is tracked with a line on the map, from Istanbul to Kathmandu, from Los Angeles to Paris.

For my husband and me, the line starts on the Central Coast, heads south to Tijuana, then south again. Our road runs along the coast, then dives into the desert, brushing past cacti and rugged mountains. We plan to follow the map, find surfing, camping, and whatever it is about this place that makes some people escape there, year after year. Whatever it is that makes others go and vow never to return.

"

The roads are notoriously narrow, winding, and spattered with semis whose drivers never seem to slow. Never drive at night, some people say. Others say never drive, period.

Friends give us things: guidebooks with shopping lists and gas receipts written inside the front cover, a piece of Astroturf to lay out behind the truck so that we'll have a dirt-free patch to sit on. Everything goes into the truck, all these pieces from people who have been before us. Even the truck itself is a gift, an old Ford that was once my father's. That slowly moving line is us, a blue truck packed full and riding low, starting down the coast.

Right before we cross the border, we fill up on gas, get pesos, and feel like we're sucking in air before we dive in. Suddenly, the freeway turns into a pinball machine, and we are rolling through, under a sign that says NO RETURN TO USA.

Ten minutes into Tijuana, we're stopped at a dusty hill-top checkpoint. All of the guards look under 20 and carry guns as long as their arms slung across their chests.

We'd been told to bring gum, or candy, or magazines to give the guards as a show of goodwill. Instead, our dog becomes our ambassador. At first, it's the guards who seem intimidated—his dark coat makes his teeth look bigger and whiter, and he's 75 pounds of restless wiggle. Then, we tell him to sit, to lie down. He obliges. Someone whispers, *He's a Hollywood dog.* While two of them glance inside the truck, one guard absent-mindedly reaches down to scratch Finn's ears.

Along the coast road to Ensenada, candy-colored hotels sprout next to corrugated metal shelters. A cruise ship floats outside of Ensenada's harbor like a giant cloud and people crowd the streets, trying to flag us into their restaurants as we drive by. After this, the road quiets. We pass a tiny chapel on a hill, painted turquoise; kids pouring out of school buses; a boy riding a circus bike with a seat taller than himself.

Odometer: 61386

When we arrive at the sandy campground next to the beach in San Quintín, it's nearly dark. An elegant older man with a white cowboy hat drives up in a black '58 Ford brimming with chrome. We admire his truck and then ask where he wants us to camp. *Anywhere you like*, he tells us, spreading his arms wide, and then he's off, driving through the campground, his tiny dust-colored dog running alongside him.

We climb out of our tent before the sun rises as a fishing family launches its boat. We roll into El Rosario an hour later and see a place that's circled on our map. At Mama Espinoza's, we opt for breakfast—chilaquiles, huevos rancheros, corn tortillas—instead of fish tacos or the famous lobster burritos.

The restaurant's walls are crowded with photos of cars and drivers who have raced the Baja 1000, an off-road race far wilder that our trip down the paved Transpeninsular Highway.

It's the diving-off point here—the next sizeable town is more than 200 slow miles away, and the landscape changes from the coastal views of the previous day to unending views of desert. Strange tall trees, resembling stick figures drawn in crayon, appear on the hillside—cirios, or boojum trees. Stout barrel cactus, even stouter boulders, yucca, cardón. At first I read off the names in one of our guidebooks, but as the miles drip by, we drive in silence, the noise of the engine only changing as Chris brakes for cows that amble across the road. I start seeing a mirage of a cow in the road in the distance.

Ever since El Rosario, our guidebooks have gotten vaguer, the distances confusing, the notes on our maps less frequent, less legible.

We follow one scrawled note and then we see posted signs with distances that don't seem to match the dusty road, toward a fishing camp near Santa Rosalilita. In the early afternoon, we bounce up and down a wretched dirt track and emerge on a hilltop. Below us, a cluster of palapas, partially walled shelters, sits at one end of an empty beach.

It's late spring: little chance of catching the west-northwest swell needed to create consistent surf, but we take out the surfboards anyway and catch a few knee-high waves built up by the wind.

The poor surf means we have the place to ourselves. Mornings, before the wind wakes up, we paddle our stand-up surfboard across the clear water. We swing in the hammock, hike in the heat to rocky coves filled with aquamarine water, fly a kite, read novels, and paint with watercolor as the sun sets.

In the evenings, we talk with a couple that lives down the road who are de facto caretakers for the camp. Over beers, the man shows us his collection of arrowheads and fossils that he's found in the hills. Each night, we go to bed feeling wind-scoured, but the back of the truck feels cozy, even as it hums like a seashell in the wind.

One day, as I paddle in to shore from the center of the small bay, two fishermen motor through in their panga. By the time I land on the beach, we have a sea bass for dinner.

One of the caretakers passes by on his way back from checking on a sailor, stranded during the month's highest tide. He asks us where we're headed next. When we tell him we're not sure, he thinks a moment, then squats down in the dirt. He has a beer in one hand; with the other, he draws a map that will take us farther south.

Odometer: 61803

At the turnoff from Highway 1, the sign reads Punta Abreojos, 63 km. In ten minutes, we pass another sign—the town is somehow farther than it was before. We spend the night by an estuary, waking in the morning to paddle through mangroves and look down through clear water at the flatfish that skim the sandy bottom. Two young girls latch onto our dog and throw a tennis ball for him, over and over. Then, it's my surf wax they want to touch and smell—it smells like bubble gum, I tell them. They ball small pieces of it in their fingers and run away, sniffing their hands.

By mid-morning, we're at the break near the small town of Abreojos. Our truck is perched on a sandy rim above the water next to faded Airstream trailers and tent campers. But there's hardly anyone in the water.

A man rolls up on a quad bike and introduces himself, his smile showing a glint of gold.

Martín is a local lobster fisherman—and surfer—and tells us that in the afternoon, the surf will pick up, the rocks will vanish under a rising tide. We sit and have a beer with him and learn about his family, his town.

He's right: The surf does pick up, but so does the wind. We huddle together inside the truck as kiteboarders use the wind to charge through the surf. One loses his board, and everyone on shore watches as he gives up and begins to swim in, his board drifting out to sea.

Another kiteboarder, watching from shore, comes over to talk with us, looking at our surfboards, still strapped on the roof of the truck. There's a place you should go, he tells us, a perfect wave that breaks for so long that the walk back along the sand once took him fifteen minutes. Then he squats down on the sand and begins to draw a line.

Odometer: Spinning

The road back from anywhere always seems like an accordion of time—flowing more quickly, as I can judge the distance from one spot to the next because I've traveled this way before; and also, more slowly, because I know exactly how many hours it is until we pass the truck with the gas can, the boulders and boojum trees, the chiles rellenos at Mama Espinoza's that won't come until late afternoon.

We pass the time by listening to old spy novels, by talking about the past—like how to construct the best mixed tape for a high school crush (the serious "I love you," we determine, is Peter Gabriel's "In Your Eyes"). And talking about the future: how our children won't even know what a mixed tape is.

Odometer: 62393

Sun, stars, smells. The magnetic field of the earth. These are things that migrating birds may use to chart their journeys. Here at the Tijuana Estuary, 370 different bird species follow their own maps to pass through, at one time or another, every year.

The area, a combination of state park, wildlife refuge national research reserve, leans on the edge of the border between Tijuana and the southern reaches of San Diego. Now in California, we can look back to the border we crossed ten days ago and see the matchbox buildings on Tijuana's hills, the giant bull ring.

Phillip Roullard, who has worked in the estuary for more than two decades, takes us along the paths, handing out sunscreen and binoculars, encouraging us to taste lemonade berry, lean closely over spittle bugs and a silvery *Argiope* spider. He's met birders from Europe who've traveled here in hopes of glimpsing the refuge's endangered birds, like the light-footed clapper rail, which builds its nest among the cordgrass.

As we walk back to the visitor's center, I spot a bird perched on the edge of the creek and pull up the binoculars to look, even though it's not so far away. Long neck, red eyes, pale feathers in a streak along its head—it's a yellow-crowned night-heron, munching on a crayfish. A migrant from Baja, Roullard says, a rare one that doesn't often come through. I think of the bird, soaring over the coastline. Did it see the sun setting in the west, a man in a white cowboy hat, our overloaded truck making its way down unfamiliar roads? Maybe it followed a constellation I couldn't identify, a smell I'll never know.

Odometer: 61821

This is what I can tell you. There is a dirt road that leads inland and then along the sea. There's a small bluff, overlooking the waves. There's our truck on the bluff, and there's Martín again, who shows up in the afternoon after we've surfed for hours: another beer, another conversation.

If you were there at night, maybe you would know the place by the moon, high in the sky a few hours before dawn, and the light of a lobster boat with a new friend in it, circling offshore. At sunrise, you would see two surfers in the water, with dolphins in between them, each telling the other that they wanted just one more long, perfect wave before they had to go.

If you still can't find it, that's all right. Put away that guidebook, with its lists of cities and shrines. There are other landmarks: some look like mileposts; some taste like fish, fresh from the sea. One of mine is the gold tooth in the smile of a lobsterman, one is the feel of salt and sand rimmed around my eyes. But if this isn't what you find, don't worry—you will know your own landmarks. In the meantime, come over here, sit down next to me, there's plenty of dirt to draw a map.

Looking In

I REMEMBER THE DAY the horses arrived. It had been raining, and for two kids cooped up inside, the afternoon seemed to stretch into years.

And then there were horses. Some were dark as thunderclouds, some roan, some palomino. There were wild mustangs and Icelandic horses with manes like clouds. My best friend and I picked each name—there was Stormlight, that one's Mackintosh—as they came down the hall.

There was also one with a rainbow coat. Another had an eggplant-colored mane. A few could even fly.

As you might have guessed, these horses weren't something anyone else could see. Only the two of us watched them canter along the nubby hallway carpet. We'd been kept inside, away from the empty lot behind my friend's back fence, where we had a world called Orak. There, dwarves crouched in tree stumps and elves reached into their quivers for silver arrows. Now our world had come to us.

I've always thought worldplay like this was something modern—which seems ridiculous, now that I think about it, because why would people in the past have smaller boundaries on their imaginations? (And it's not like I was terribly original, either, with most of my ideas coming from already-created lands like Narnia and Middle Earth, the World of Two Moons and Camelot).

People have been creating imaginary worlds for millennia. Aristotle wrote about the art of memory, and others in ancient Greece and Rome elaborated, discussing the creation of what became known as memory palaces, real or imagined places that can store information in the mind.

That's what got Jacob Levernier, then a doctoral student at the University of Oregon, interested in the imaginary worlds. He'd been studying psychology and medieval philosophy as an undergraduate and learned about memory palaces of the past. In the Middle Ages, monks used the architecture of their imaginations to store scripture and teachings. They also simulated experiences in their minds that would help them, for example, act in a more moral way in different situations, as well as instructing others in these practices.

The Reformation put a damper on memory palaces, but imaginary worlds continued to appear in literature and art. Writers and artists from the Brontë sisters and C.S. Lewis to Fairfield Porter and Claes Oldenberg constructed their own lands as children.

Today, kids tend to make imaginary friends between four and six years of age; imaginary worlds began to be constructed between eight and 12. While studies suggest that anywhere from a third to three-quarters of young children are playing with imaginary friends, imaginary worlds are rarer.

It's estimated that three to 12 percent of children create imaginary worlds, yet "no one's really asked children about this," Levernier says. "We're wondering if imaginary worlds might be the next step in complex creative play."

Past studies of imaginary worlds have focused on adults recalling the childhood worlds they created. Michele Root-Bernstein, a creativity scholar who is adjunct faculty at Michigan State University, sent questionnaires to MacArthur fellows about imaginary worlds. She also polled MSU students about imaginary worlds and their current courses of study and career aspirations.

Root-Bernstein found that while previous studies suggested that those who played in imaginary worlds displayed artistic sensibilities that might foreshadow a career in the arts, MacArthur fellows in both sciences and the arts played in imaginary worlds as children. While students were less likely than the fellows to have had imaginary worlds as children, students who did came from all fields as well.

For many of the fellows Root-Bernstein studied, worldplay continued into their adult lives in one form or another. Some who had pursued sciences talked about how creating hypotheses was a form of invention that had similar qualities to their early worldplay.

Several of the fellows, in fact, still returned occasionally to their childhood worlds—and also expressed embarrassment about doing so.

Before starting to read about imaginary worlds, I'd thought little of Orak and the other games I once played. Once puberty hit, I packed them all away somewhere. My best friend and I drifted apart as our imagined worlds faded, too.

But ever since I started thinking about imaginary worlds again a few weeks ago, I feel lighter somehow. I already go to plenty of places in my mind—to frightening imaginary worlds where I can't pay my bills and lose the house, to smaller ones in which I deflect the rude customer in front of me in line with a clever turn of phrase or say the perfect comforting words I wish I'd thought of to a friend. In fact, I do this so much that I sometimes act out these conversations. It's only when my husband sighs and says, "What are you rehashing now?" that I realize my mouth is moving and my hands are waving in the air.

One idea that researchers are pursuing is that imaginary worlds might be a place for children to practice verbal and social skills, among other things. At this point, I don't know if revisiting these past worlds of mine can help me much. So instead of going to the world of the crowded post office, or to the telephone call with the editor, why not to somewhere I can hear hooves in full gallop against the cobblestone? A place where the wind rushes past my ears and I put my face close to a mane of clouds and ride.

Egg Drop

THIS WEEKEND my oldest son held two brown eggs in his hand. He cradled them gently. Then he threw one on the ground. It bounced, and he laughed. This one was rubber. The other egg he held was a real one.

I've never gotten used to the fake egg. Sometimes it appears in egg cartons. Other times, it's lonely in the corner of the room. But mostly, it gets thrown. It's the most realistic I've ever seen, the perfect oval, the exact mix of brown and a bit of pink.

In real eggs, the shade of the shell comes from a mix of just two pigments, a blue-green and a brown-red. Birds can produce a rainbow of colors from this pair, whether robin's blue or the brick red of a Cetti's warbler. And it's likely that this color appears quite close to the time an egg is released. There are many ideas about the reason behind different hue—it can be camouflage, a sign of health, a protection from UV light, a way of sneaking additional eggs into a surrogate parent's nest.

The shape of eggs is something people have pondered, too. There are elegant ovals, jellybeans, ping-pong balls, and a range of forms in between. In the past, people had proposed multiple reasons for different egg shapes—could it be where they build their nests, or how many eggs they need to fit? But after looking at the egg shapes of 1,400 bird species, researchers found that egg shape is related to flight. Birds that are known for their flight skills tend to lay eggs that their light-boned, streamlined bodies can accommodate—these eggs are longer and more elliptical. Birds that cover smaller distances, under lower power, tend to lay more rounded eggs. The researchers have said that if you give them an egg, they could make a good guess about how well the bird flies.

This sort of prediction reminds me of the things people used to say about the shape of my pregnant belly. *It's high and sticking out like a submarine—must be a boy. It's a girl, or else you wouldn't be carrying so low. I wouldn't know you were pregnant from the back—boy. I'd know you were pregnant just looking at your face.* I felt pulled in so many directions—I desperately wanted to know exactly what this person would be, and I also didn't want anyone else to tell me.

There's still so much we don't know about the shape of an egg, and what's inside it. It's possible that increasing the elliptical shape of an egg was an evolutionary solution to allow for a larger embryo without increasing the width of the egg. There's also more to learn about what it looks like—some birds have eggs with intricate patterns on the shell, others have brightly colored eggs that are billboards to a predator on their unprotected nests on the ground.

Even when we guess right, there's always something else that we don't account for to lead us to wherever we're headed next. With my son, I've started trying to keep a poker face when he asks me to catch an egg. Tonight, when I asked him what his next step in trickery might be, he thought about it

a moment. Then he said he might walk or run with his egg
and pretend to trip.

A long time ago, the eggshell was a source of strength—
it's what gave reptiles the safety to reproduce on land. Still,
when I think of one falling, I can't help trying to reach for
it. Those beautiful, fragile eggs.

Fruit Fly Walks into a Bar

WHEN I LIVED in Madrid in college, I read several guide-book descriptions of Café Gijón and knew I had to go. I wasn't sure if I was going to be a writer, but I sure liked the *idea* of being a writer, and a "famous literary café" with artists and writers still meeting up to drink and philosophize sounded like somewhere I needed to be.

I showed up one winter afternoon, ordered a coffee in my shy Spanish, and waited. When nothing happened but the arrival of my coffee, I didn't know what to do, so I pulled out a notebook and began to write.

What happened next might be a little blurred by years and vino tinto, but suddenly there was a balding man sitting across from me holding out a tiny glass of sherry. I found myself trying to tell him about the one philosophically oriented book I'd read recently, *The Quantum Society*, but I got mixed up somewhere between the particles and the waves.

Whatever I said must have sounded as bad as that does, because he said, "You're not very articulate. But you're still very young. Why don't you come sit with my friends?"

I started thinking about this night when I was sitting in a bar a few weeks ago at a table of strangers. The occasion was a science pub night, part of a monthly series of talks put on by our town's natural history museum.

Before I went, I figured the attendees would be a small, older crowd—you know, museum donors, retirees, volunteer docents. But the bar tables were packed, even the pool tables had been turned into beer-friendly surfaces, and my table had a range of ages and backgrounds—an accountant, a university employee, some guys from a local software company.

Alison Pischedda, the researcher who gave the talk, started out the night by saying that there'd be a fair amount of sex and sperm in her talk, billed as "Sperm Wars and Sexual Conflict"—"so if that makes you uncomfortable, you might want to get another beer." And the photos and videos she showed—one included a hermaphroditic flatworm sucking undesirable sperm out after a session in a flatworm mating ring—set off slightly boozy laughter. But at the end of the talk, people asked questions about the proteins in *Drosophila* semen that can affect female behavior. They asked how female eggs might be evolving, about the logistics of conducting experiments with fruit flies, about the problem of anthropomorphizing when part of your research is about sex.

Years ago, in Café Gijón, I sat around a table with a group of writers, straining to understand as they argued and interrupted each other and ordered more wine and coffee. Since then, I've often wished that gatherings like these were a more regular part of my life. I've wondered what it would have been like to step into an English coffeehouse in its heyday. I might have watched Sir Isaac Newton and Edmund Halley dissect a dolphin right inside The Grecian, or hear sailors and scientists learn from each other at The Marine. (Of course, I probably would have needed to attend disguised as a man, but since this is my daydream and not day-to-day reality, the intrigue adds to the appeal).

For Pischedda, the appeal of doing an informal talk like the one I went to is the chance to return to the questions that originally hooked her into evolutionary biology. "When you study fruit flies, like I do, people don't always get why you're doing that," she said. Talks like this can help people understand more about what she's investigating.

I only went to Café Gijón once. I think I didn't want to go back until I could offer something too, until I could argue and interrupt and order more wine and coffee. And now that I think about it, all the learning and talking and reading and writing I've done since has, on some level, been a way of readying myself to return.

What's My Lipstick?

The rumors are true: I'm kind of a slob. In high school, I wore baggy pants during the day and boxer shorts to volleyball practice. In college, I wore pajama bottoms to morning classes. I also wore them at least once to an afternoon coffee that turned out to be a date.

And more recently, at a wonderfully dirty camp in the mountains, a friend and I were talking about what we wore when we took the kids to school. I looked down at my holey yoga pants and my sweatshirt and my dusty running shoes and said that I looked like this pretty much all the time.

So when I heard about enclothed cognition, I was intrigued. In 2012, researchers coined the term to mean how clothes influence the wearer's psychology. They looked at how wearing a lab coat affected students' performance on a test that measured their attention. If the students were told the coat was a doctor's coat, and wore it while taking the test, they showed greater attention than if they merely saw the coat—or if they wore the coat but were told it was a painter's coat.

The researchers write that the effect may come from two different things: what the clothes symbolize and how the person feels when she wears them. Several studies show similar connections between clothes and how they make us feel and think. A series of five studies suggested that formal clothing enhances the ability to think abstractly. Formal clothing, the researchers say, can increase the social or psychological distance between people. This distance can increase abstract thinking—when events are psychologically closer, they're thought of more concretely.

That might be part of why I have trouble dressing up—it does feel like it creates an awkward space bubble between me and everyone else. (Three-day-old yoga pants could do that, too). And this spring, I felt isolated no matter what clothes I was wearing. I was going through a blue period that involved more than just the navy 15-year-old sweatshirt of my husband's that I wore most days.

My mom reminded me of my fabulously dressed aunt's advice for times like these: just slap on your lipstick and go out and face the world. *But I don't WEAR lipstick*, I said. What could I do instead? Take a shower? Put on clean yoga pants? Lace up my running shoes?

What I did eventually was get help. And I started feeling better.

There was something else, too. It was one of my lowest days, when I just put on the clothes that I'd piled on the chair the night before, or maybe they were even the clothes I slept in. I still had to take my son to school. On our way into the building, the two of us started walking behind another mom who clearly had taken her time to pick out new clothes, to brush her hair, to put on her makeup.

There was a time when I would have thought something like this: *How frivolous. What a waste of time to spend on something that's just about appearances.* That day, seeing this woman in the sunlight, holding her child's hand, a different feeling washed over me: respect. *How honorable*, I remember thinking. I didn't know anything about this woman—who she was, where she was going next, what else was happening in her life—but she took care with herself. It is an honorable thing, to take that kind of care.

That morning, I pulled up my hoodie and slouched back to the van. I still don't wear lipstick. But the next morning, I got up and put on my jeans.

*Orchid Care
for the Uncertain*

I WAKE UP this morning on the prickly side—or at least, I'm prickly once I look at my phone. There are a series of misunderstood texts, frail disjointed things that have good intentions but poor phrasing, or lack the perfect emoji.

My phone is sitting right next to an orchid. It's a new type of orchid for me—a miltonia, with narrow leaves that point upward and a sweet, pansy-like flower. But now the orchid's flowers have withered and some of its leaves are yellowing. It may be getting too much light. It may be getting too much water, or not enough.

I thought I was doing so well with my orchids. We had received several plants as gifts; a few months ago, I decided I needed to start taking better care of the plants if I ever wanted them to flower again. I bought pots with holes to let their roots breathe. I researched the right potting mix, I unwound roots that had grown soggy. There is now a special spray bottle that I take around the house to give them a tropical misting.

The ones I've re-potted have been growing new leaves.

150

But this morning, the straw-colored tips of the miltonia leaves reminded me that I must keep taking care of things, keep learning how to take care in new ways.

Sometimes taking care of things makes me exhausted. That was the problem with all of those texts. And then my middle son wakes up prickly because we are going to church. We don't even go to church unless we're visiting a grandmother or, some years, on Christmas Eve. We've been talking about Martin Luther King Jr. Day and we don't really have a tradition to celebrate it, I tell him. Maybe going to church will be a way to do that.

He cries.

At church we sit in the back, the place for the uncertain and conscripted. We sing "Lift Every Voice and Sing," a song that usually gives me a soaring, achy feeling. This time, it's sung by an earnest choir at a different cadence than I remember. I spend most of the song both encouraged that my boys are trying to sing along and distressed that this is the version they are hearing first. This does not help with the prickliness.

I should be paying better attention. That's why we're here, after all, that's why I made us come, so that we would pay attention. Someone reads a Mary Oliver poem, "Don't Hesitate." I love Mary Oliver. I love this poem. Still, I can only concentrate on what my youngest son is doing, which is measuring our hands against each other. "Your fingers are pointy," he says. "Why are your fingers so pointy?"

The minister talks about a visit that King had made to Berlin in 1964, where King spoke about the wall that had been built three years earlier. The minister says that usually it's a fool's errand to guess what people in the past would say about the present, but she could imagine what King would say about another wall today.

I could see that my older sons had the concentrated expressions of trying to understand something that's just out of reach. I imagine the questions they will have: *Why was there a wall in Berlin? Right in the middle of the city? What would you do if your friends were on the other side? Is there a wall like that still?*

My youngest son is taking the rings off my fingers and putting them on his own small thumbs. There is a part of me that thinks I should worry about him losing them, and then the other part of me sees what he sees, how shiny they are, how they look so heavy and large and also strangely joyful on his dimpled hands.

I used to do the same thing with my dad on the occasional Sundays he went to church with the rest of the family. I remember spinning the ring around his finger, tracing the ridges on his fingernails. There was a sweet spot at the base of his thumb where the skin was especially soft. The last time I went to church with him, when I was 24 and he was 77, I held his hand and touched the same spot with my own thumb.

This morning, as the minister ends the sermon, my son replaces the rings on my finger, wraps my arms around his face so he couldn't see, then wraps them around his chest. "When is this going to be done?" he says into my ear.

My sons are surprised when the next song starts and I whisper to them that we are going to walk quietly out of the church. They ask if something is wrong. "There's nothing wrong," I say. "You did a wonderful job of listening."

Outside, the sky is gray and the magnolia tree is dark and happy with the recent rain. No one asks the questions I think they will. They ask whether eating too much fat can suffocate you, as a friend has informed them; once reassured, they ask if we can go to McDonald's.

Later, when I am considering whether to water the miltonia, what the minister said comes back to me: the fight doesn't end. We don't get to stop after just one victory, one defeat. We need to continue to risk losing who we think we are to become who the world needs us to be.

I have told myself I will never get another orchid. The plants are too much work. But then I recall how Mary Oliver writes about the possibilities that still remain, which makes me think of my dad and his greenhouse. It was filled with spider plants because he couldn't bear not to propagate the plantlets they produced. He wanted to give them possibility. Maybe I do, too: I think of the unexpected joy of removing each orchid from its too-small pot, the roots circling my fingers like rings.

Yes, We Did

CASSIE, when you proposed this series of conversations about whether or not to have a baby—well, the truth is, I was worried. There's nothing that seems to make a comments section ignite like someone pontificating on motherhood. And I'm embarrassed to say, I'm not quite sure if my—our—decision to have kids had much to do with science, beyond that biology might have conquered all.

There wasn't a particular moment that settled it. What I remember was that at some point, the if in the ongoing conversation between my husband and me turned into a cautious when.

This shift happened right around the time I turned 30. The timing was perfect. I could just tell people—I imagine I have told people, people who I didn't really want to get into it with—that it was that rhythmic ticking, insistent as the clock inside the crocodile that trailed Captain Hook in hopes of his other hand, and everything attached.

But I'm guessing that doesn't help you much. At least, when I was trying to think about what life with kids might be like, and how to make a decision about that life, that's not what I wanted to know.

154

This was not a decision I made rationally. The truth is (and I can't believe I'm admitting it in front of you) it mostly had to do with feelings, with memories. Even with poetry.

One of these feelings: how loved I felt as a kid. I always knew my parents were crazy about my brother and me. My dad, in particular—he was 50 when he met my mom, and at that point, I don't think he thought he would ever have a family.

I couldn't figure out exactly what we were doing to be so delightful, but even at the time, I knew he thought we had changed his life for the better.

I guess another way to talk about how I made the decision is to tell you about a poem I once read. I can't remember the name of it, or who wrote it, and I might even be misremembering what it's about. But in my memory, there is a stadium filled with all of the lives that a person could have led, and they are all sitting there, watching the life you've chosen play out the rest of the game.

I first read the poem when I was in Spain and realized that the doctor that I thought I was going to be needed to step off the grass and into the stands, to watch.

And later, as my husband and I thought about having children, I realized that the game I wanted to see was the one in which a mother stood at the center of the field.

Because I knew—for me—this would be the most unpredictable life, the one that would deal out the most challenges, provide the most risk. Another person could find a cause and fight for it, move to another country, transform herself from the inside out. She could invite children into her life in other ways, and really let them in.

And this is one of my weaknesses. I'm too cautious to do any of that. I'm too happy to keep doing things the way I've always done them. Too quick to throw up very comfortable walls that keep the rest of the world out.

One of the things that I was both dreading and wishing for was exactly this: that parenthood would make me a different person. A selfless person. I had a friend who, on several occasions when I put her off by saying we were waiting a few more years to have kids, said, "So, you're just going to have a few more selfish years, then?"

After I had my first son, I found that I was a different person. And I wasn't at all. I still got hungry and grumpy and worried and tired. I still did not mind cleaning toilets, like I had in college. I still wanted nothing to do with vomit. I still looked longingly at waves I didn't have time to ride.

But new things have emerged and continue to do so. I've found I am (usually, mostly) more patient than I ever thought I could be. I can (usually, mostly) sing lullabies until my voice gets hoarse. Even though I'm not someone who would have been described as warm, nurturing, motherly—I liked it all so much (usually, mostly) that I wanted to do it again.

And here's where maybe the science part comes in. Through my children, my capacity for wonder has returned. Before they were born, I had come to a point where, even though I asked questions for a living, I had stopped asking the questions that mattered.

Now I have to answer questions from the time I wake up until long after we should all be in bed.

In answering, I realize how much I don't know. Why, for instance, is the ocean salty? How did it get salty in the first place? What is that slimy stuff coming out a snail? Why do people like shoes so much? Do monkeys sweat?

There are all the questions that I will never have the answers to: Will we all die in the same house? Where is

Grandpa Morley now? When we die, will our dishes still be here? (Actually, I can probably guess the answer to the last one: yes, there will always be dishes in the sink.)

I guess this is getting into something that you didn't ask about, which is, what was the result of all of these feelings, this poetry? For me, it's been connection. Connection with the questions that I should be asking. Connection with other parents, and with my own.

One of the great joys of being a parent has been seeing my mom being a grandmother. Seeing how she loves my sons, I can see how much she loved me as a child, how much she loves me still. I feel the same joy seeing my brother be an uncle. Seeing my husband be a father.

I realize I haven't said much about the challenges of being a parent, but it seems like enough people talk about that. There are things that I have given up, at least for the moment. But with everything I've received from my children, I feel like I'm only now entering my selfish years.

Somewhere in that stadium in the poem that may or may not exist, many people who I might have been fill the stands. At least one of them is a doctor. At least one of them is a biologist. One does research on bioluminescent plankton in Belize, another climbs into tree canopies, another works in Antarctica. Several wrote books before they turned 35. They speak many languages, and they surf more gracefully, ski more boldly, and run faster than the person standing in the center of the field.

But that's the thing: I'm not alone out there.

There are so many people with me. Some of us have kids and some don't, and some are doctors, and some are biologists, and some have written books. One of them is you. And my boys are there, too, saying that now is the time for me to play.

Loose Ends

I USUALLY AVOID talking to people at the gym. But a few weeks ago, the man next to me had his shoes untied, and I couldn't help myself. The laces were bright red, and extremely long. He was doing sidesteps that looked like they had high trip potential. And I was extra-sensitive to falls that day—my mother-in-law had ended up in the hospital after losing her footing in her backyard, and this gentleman looked about the same age, and was approaching his exercises with the same determination I imagined she would.

"Could I tie those for you?" I asked. I felt like I needed to give some sort of explanation. "I tie a lot of shoes," I said.

He laughed and thanked me. "You must have kids. I remember that," he said. "When my son was little, even if I double-knotted them, his shoes always came untied, too. I don't know how he did it."

That's the thing, we don't even have to do anything. Except move our feet. The very action of running—and also, I'd imagine, skipping, dancing, climbing up on the kitchen counter when you're not supposed to, sprinting through the library after being told not to, hurtling yourself over the guardrail at Glacier Point—creates enough force on shoelaces to make that sweet little bow you tied fall apart, sometimes in a matter of seconds. (The guardrail thing also creates enough of a squeezing force on a parent's heart to render them at first speechless, then unable to stop yelling.)

To figure this out, researchers filmed a colleague's shoes as these shoes were put through their paces on a treadmill. During the run, the shoe hits the ground with seven times the force of gravity, and that force stretches and relaxes the knot, which can begin to wiggle free. As the foot swings to recover and take the next step, the shoelaces whip around, creating inertial forces on the lace. Combined with the loosening knot, the laces fly free. Watching the movements in slow motion, the researchers found that this can all happen in two strides.

But sometimes, laces really do stay tied all day. The researchers aren't sure why. What they do know is that the moment the knot starts to falter, it can cause "an avalanche of failure," one said.

They have looked into it further, adding weights at the ends of laces, trying different lengths and styles of laces. One of their interests is in DNA and other microstructures, determining what forces could make them fail and what arrangements make them resist detangling.

With shoes, there is a way to tie a single knot that makes it less likely to fail. The reef knot, or square knot, holds laces more securely than the granny knot. The easy give-away is that if you tie your laces and the bow turns so that it runs along your shoe, rather than across the top of your shoe, you're likely tying a granny knot.

I still remember the feeling of someone else tying my shoe. It feels secure, comforting. Even the rhythm of it, the words you learn as you are taught how to tie it. The rabbit goes around the tree, under the hole, and out the other side.

Right over left, left over right, makes this knot both tidy and tight. I can see my neighbor bent over my small sneakers, showing me the rabbit. I can remember my dad's hands as he tugged at the ends of my laces.

Now I am the one tying, the one teaching. Rabbits, rhymes, I'll say anything if it helps keep everything together. Maybe I should be saying something to myself: with this knot, I am trying to stop the avalanche of failure. Even though I know nothing can stop it.

The man with the bright red laces knew this. "Are you sure I can't help?" I asked him.

"Oh, no," he said, smiling. "They'll just come untied again anyway." And then he sidestepped merrily away, his laces slithering along behind him.

Maybe More Than You Wanted to Know About Hearts

SOMEHOW I ALWAYS knew there was something about my dad's heart. I'm not sure exactly what I knew, but I did know that he didn't eat certain things, like eggs and bacon, and ate other things, like canned tuna and low-fat cheese and margarine. (It was the eighties). He enrolled in a cholesterol study. Bottles of liquid meals appeared in the fridge, all autumn-colored: pale orange and green and brown.

I knew enough—or at least, I was worried enough—to read the sign at the waterpark where we'd climbed up to the top of the slide. I was small, and scared, but I told him he shouldn't go down. It wasn't good for people with heart problems. The heart seemed like a frightening thing, or at least unruly, ready to misbehave at any minute, something that constantly needed watching.

I feel less watchful now, but I do find myself drawn to any information about the heart. To the blue whale, its 400-pound heart as big as a Harley-Davidson, working to its edge. When it dives, it drops its heart rate from around 30 beats per minute to four.

I find how we talk about the heart fascinating, too. We are disheartened, we have lost heart, and it is hard to go on. The hearts of those we love are sweet. The ones we don't, or who don't love us, we call heartless. A different way of being without a heart. There are many creatures that never have a heart at all. The sea cucumbers, the jellies, the sea stars, the flatworms. And then there are the cephalopods, which have three. Two hearts do their work for the gills, the other sends blue blood swooshing to the organs. An octopus's organ-focused heart even stops while it swims.

Hearts seem like small animals. They leap and flutter and sink. They can be heavy, they can be light. In Etruscan shrews, they can race along at 1,500 beats per minute. The lowest heart rate observed during a blue whale's dive was two beats per minute.

Beat.

Count slowly to 30.

Beat.

If you think of someone who is all heart, do you imagine them as a four-chambered organ, the size of a fist? Does it surprise you that dogs' hearts make up a bigger portion of their mass than almost all other animals?

And then there are trees. They have no wet engine, but the central column of wood that supports them is called the duramen, the heartwood. It will not falter if the surrounding layers of living tissue and the bark keep it safe. This heart is at the center of things, even though in most of us it sits slightly to the left. We can transplant hearts back into the body's soil.

The heart of the matter, the heart of the problem. We get to the heart of it. We steal hearts and we take heart and we wear them on our sleeves. We open our hearts, we close them. Inside, the valves open and close, too, letting blood rush in and rush back out again. Although we have only one, we can lose them again and again. I sometimes imagine hearts scattered about the world like lost socks. Where do they all gather? Is there somewhere that they find each other, scattered in the gutter or clumped at the storm drain?

Wherever they go, they contain both movement and sound, a marker of time, if time is something that can be marked. The clock before there was a clock. Maybe hearts are time themselves. We don't know how many heartbeats we have, but there is this one, and this one, and this one. Sometimes they murmur. Sometimes they pound.

It is better, though, if it is not always steady. Better to have a tripping rhythm that speeds up and slows down with every breath. A new type of pacemaker will even listen to the heart and follow its irregular lead, a willing dance partner from tango to foxtrot to TikTok mashup. The heart might march to the beat of its own drum, but when people sing together in groups, their breathing and their heartbeats start to synchronize.

It was my dad's heart in the end. It stopped, and then it was restarted, but the rest of him never resurfaced alongside it. Then, eventually, his heart stopped for good. It is easy to say it was his heart, because it feels like it's all of our hearts, always up to something: aching and soaring, growing cold, starting to thaw. A zebrafish can repair its own heart, but to fix our hearts, sometimes we need each other. We need someone whose heart goes out to our lost ones and brings them skipping back home.

Notes

Looking Up

Auditing Astronomy Class

"I listened to one of his lectures": Lectures from Dr. Filippenko's Fall 2006 Introduction to General Astronomy course are available at https://archive.org/details/ucberkeley_webcast_itunesu_461110233.

"Steve Weinberg (don't know who he is)": Steven Weinberg was a theoretical physicist who won the Nobel Prize in Physics in 1979.

Window Seat

"The first book about writing that I read": Anne Lamott, *Bird by Bird* (New York: Pantheon, 1994).

"wonderful things with a limited view": Elisabeth Tova Bailey, *The Sound of a Wild Snail Eating* (Chapel Hill: Algonquin Books, 2010).

"the person who makes Harry Potter feel like he has a family": JK Rowling, *Harry Potter and the Prisoner of Azkaban* (London: Bloomsbury, 1999).

Moonstruck

"On the nights of brightest moonlight, these calls and flashes increase": Vincenzo Penteriani et al., "Moonlight makes owls more chatty," *PLoS ONE* 5:1, e8696. (2010), doi:10.1371/journal.pone.0008696

A. Roger Ekirch, *At Day's Close: Night in Times Past* (New York: Norton, 2005).

"Pliny the Elder observed": Pliny the Elder, *Natural History* (John Bostock, M.D., F.R.S., H.T. Riley, Esq., B.A. London. Taylor and Francis, Red Lion Court, Fleet Street. 1855). Available online http://www.perseus.tufts.edu/hopper/text?doc=Perseus:text:1999.02.0137

"Bos and a colleague made more than 100 visits": Arthur R. Bos and Girley S. Gumanao, "The lunar cycle determines availability of coral-reef fishes at fish markets," *Journal of Fish Biology* 81:6 (2012), 2074–9.

"He found that both wild dogs and cheetahs": "Fear of the Dark or Dinner by Moonlight? Reduced Temporal Partitioning among Africa's Large Carnivores," *Ecology*, 93:12 (2012), 2590–99.

"they found a gene encoding a coral cryptochrome": O. Levy et al., "Light-responsive cryptochromes from a simple multicellular animal, the coral Acropora millepora," *Science* 318:5849 (2007), 467–70. doi: 10.1126/science.1145432

"Galapagos marine iguanas travel from their resting spots": M. Wikelski, and M. Hau, "Is there an endogenous tidal foraging rhythm in marine iguanas?" *Journal of Biological Rhythms* 10:4 (1995), 335–50. doi: 10.1177/074873049501000407

"Because they did see entanglement": Christian Cajochen et al., "Evidence that the lunar cycle influences human sleep," *Current Biology* 23:15 (2013), 1485–8. doi: 10.1016/j.cub.2013.06.029

"My friend who's an emergency room nurse": thank you, Harmonie Sykes, for years of steady and steadying friendship.

View from Above

"an essay by the commander's son, Evan.": Evan Hadfield, *The Globe and Mail*, December 18, 2012.

OCEAN VIEW

Psyche and the Seashore

"Psychologist Shigehiro Oishi worked with a group of students": S. Oishi, T. Talhelm, & M. Lee, "Personality and geography: Introverts prefer mountains," *Journal of Research in Personality* 58 (2015), 55–68. doi:10.1016/j.jrp.2015.07.001

Susan Cain, *Quiet: The Power of Introverts in a World That Can't Stop Talking.* (New York: Crown, 2012).

"When I asked a group of writers": Thank you, writers of SciLance!

The Sadness of Solving a Mystery

"affixed transmitters to the feathers of three of Taiaroa Head's fledglings": Bindi (Thomas) Robertson, Edward Minot, & J.D. Holland, "Fledging behaviour of juvenile northern royal albatrosses (Diomedea sanfordi): A GPS tracking study," *Notornis* 57 (2010), 135–147.

"wanted to learn more about these young loggerheads' early travels": Katherine Mansfield et al., "First satellite tracks of neonate sea turtles redefine the 'lost years' oceanic niche," *Proceedings. Biological sciences/The Royal Society* 281:20133039 (2014). doi:10.1098/rspb.2013.3039.

Helen Rozwadowski, *Fathoming the Ocean: The Discovery and Exploration of the Deep Sea* (Boston: Belknap Press, 2005).

Lonely Abalone

Daniel L. Geiger & Buzz Owen. *Abalone: Worldwide Haliotidae.* (Hackenhein, Germany: ConchBooks, 2012).

"sending messages in bottles": Neil Gaiman, commencement address at the University of Arts, May 17, 2012. https://www.uarts.edu/neil-gaiman-keynote-address-2012

Grunion Run

"a new paper by Martin, Studer, and their colleagues": Karen Martin et al., "Population trends of beach-spawning California grunion Leuresthes tenuis monitored by citizen scientists," *ICES Journal of Marine Science* 77:6 (2019), 2226–2233. doi:10.1093/icesjms/fsz086.

MARVELOUS CREATURES

Alligator Awesome

Diane Kelly, "Penile Anatomy and Hypotheses of Erectile Function in the American Alligator (*Alligator mississippiensis*): Muscular Eversion and Elastic Retraction," *Anatomical Record*, 296 (2013), 488–494. doi:10.1002/ar.22644

If You Feed Them, They Will Come

"researchers tracked the movements of several tourist-fed rays": M. Corcoran, et al., "Supplemental feeding for ecotourism reverses diel activity and alters movement patterns and spatial distribution of the southern stingray, *Dasyatis americana*," *PLOS ONE* (2013). doi:10.1371/journal.pone.0059235

"June Dwyer . . . highlighted the human desire to connect with animals throughout Western literature": June Dwyer, "Do Not Feed the Animals: Do Not Touch: Desire for Wild Animal Companionship in the Twenty-first Century," *Interdisciplinary Studies in Literature and Environment* 19:4 (2012), 623–644. https://www.jstor.org/stable/44087159

Wallace J. Nichols, *Blue Mind: The Surprising Science That Shows How Being near, in, on, or under Water Can Make You Happier, Healthier, More Connected and Better at What You Do.* (New York: Little, Brown and Company, 2014).

Snail Season

University of California Division of Agriculture and Natural Resources Integrated Pest Management. *"Snails and Slugs."* http://ipm.ucanr.edu/PMG/PESTNOTES/pn7427.html

Knight Moves

"which some trace to more than a thousand years ago in India," as well as an invaluable resource for general theory and description of the Knight's Tour: George Jelliss, "Knight's Tour Notes." http://www.mayhematics.com/t/t.htm

"A list of descriptions of a knight's movement": As cited by Edward Winter (1998) in *The Knight's Challenge.* https://www.chesshistory.com/winter/extra/knight.html

"Mathematicians and computer scientists are interested": e.g., Shun-Shii Lin and Chung-Liang Wei, "Optimal algorithms for constructing knight's tours on arbitrary n×m chessboards," *Discrete Applied Mathematics* 146: 3 (2005), 219–232. doi:10.1016/j.dam.2004.11.002

WEATHER WATCHING

June Gloom

"perhaps it's a victory that the fog is still there at all": Alicia Toregrosa, Travis O'Brien, and Ian Faloona, "Coastal fog, climate change, and the environment," *Eos Trans. AGU*, 95:50 (2014), 473–474. doi:10.1002/2014EO500001

Bob Berwyn, David Hasemyer, Mallory Pickett, "With a warming climate, coastal fog around the world is declining," *Inside Climate News*, October 10, 2021.

Water Year

"*The National Weather Service used to use the rainfall year*": Joseph Serna, "Ideologies clash as weather service realigns the annual rainfall calendar," *Los Angeles Times*, July 2, 2015.

ON THE LAND

Taking the High Road

John Muir quotation: First published as "In the Yosemite: Holidays Among the Rocks," *New York Tribune*, January 1, 1872. Later published as "Yosemite in Winter"

"*the Sierra Club is now working to address this part of its history*": Michael Brune. "Pulling Down Our Monuments." *SierraClub.org*, July 22, 2020. https://www.sierraclub.org/michael-brune/2020/07/john-muir-early-history-sierra-club

Howard Weamer. *The Perfect Art: The Ostrander Hut and Ski Touring in Yosemite.* (Self-published, 1995).

Depth Afield

Martha Sandweiss. *Print the Legend: Photography and the American West.* (New Haven: Yale University Press, 2002).

Landscape Poetry

Tom Killion. *California's Wild Edge: The Coast in Prints, Poetry, and History.* (Berkeley: Heyday Books, 2015).

Rainbow Connection

"*According to one botanist*": "Rainbow in a Tree," Andrew P. Han, *Science Friday*, November 6, 2013. https://www.sciencefriday.com/articles/rainbow-in-a-tree/

Can 58,800+ Lights Help Us See What's Right in Front of Us?

"*At a 2014 conference at UC Santa Cruz, Ursula K. LeGuin gave a talk*": LeGuin was speaking at Anthropocene: Arts of Living on a Damaged Planet. https://www.youtube.com/watch?v=6BW8YmRAoW4

LOOKING IN

Brave New Worlds

Taylor, Levernier, and their colleagues published some of their work on imaginary worlds following my conversation with Levernier: Marjorie Taylor et al., "Paracosms: The Imaginary Worlds of Middle Childhood," *Child Development* 91 (2018). doi:10.1111/cdev.13162.

"sent questionnaires to MacArthur fellows about imaginary worlds": Michele Root-Bernstein, and Robert Root-Bernstein,"Imaginary Worldplay in Childhood and Maturity and Its Impact on Adult Creativity," *Creativity Research Journal* 18:4 (2006), 405–425.

Egg Drop

"this color appears quite close to the time an egg is released": Pat Leonard, "The Beauty and Biology of Egg Color," *The Cornell Lab: All About Birds,* June 12, 2017. https://www.allaboutbirds.org/news/the-beauty-and-biology-of-egg-color/

"egg shape is related to flight": Mary Caswell Stoddard et al., "Avian egg shape: Form, function, and evolution," *Science* 356:6344 (2017), 1249–1254. doi:10.1126/science.aaj1945

What's My Lipstick?

"In 2012, researchers coined the term [enclothed cognition]": Hajo Adam & Adam Galinsky, "Enclothed cognition," *Journal of Experimental Social Psychology,* 48:4 (2012), 918–925. doi:10.1016/j.jesp.2012.02.008

"A series of five studies suggested that formal clothing enhances the ability to think abstractly": Michael L. Slepian et al., "The Cognitive Consequences of Formal Clothing," *Social Psychological and Personality Science* 6:6 (2015), 661–668. doi:0.1177/1948550615579462

Loose Ends

"researchers filmed a colleague's shoes": C.A. Daily-Diamond et al., "The roles of impact and inertia in the failure of a shoelace knot," *Proc Math Phys Eng Sci* 473 (2017). doi:10.1098/rspa.2016.0770

Maybe More Than You Wanted to Know About Hearts

"When it dives, it drops its heart rate from 30 beats per minute to four": J.A. Goldbogen et al., "Extreme bradycardia and tachycardia in the

world's largest animal," *Proc Natl Acad Sci* 116:50 (2019), 25329–25332. doi:10.1073/pnas.1914273116

"There are creatures that never have a heart at all": A. Alibhai et al., "Hearts, and the Heartless, in the Animal Kingdom," Frontiers for Young Minds, October 2, 2020. https://kids.frontiersin.org/articles/10.3389/frym.2020.540440

"wet engine": This essay, and this writer, are inspired by the writings of Brian Doyle, whose essay "Joyas Voldadoras" (American Scholar, 2012) and book *The Wet Engine* (Massachusetts: Paraclete Press, 2005) are only two of his many works on the mystery and wonder of the heart.

"A new type of pacemaker": J. Shanks et al., "Reverse re-modelling chronic heart failure by reinstating heart rate variability," *Basic Research in Cardiology*, 117:1 (2022) doi:10.1007/s00395-022-00911-0

"When people sing together in groups, their heartbeats can synchronize": B. Vickhoff et al., "Music structure determines heart rate variability of singers," *Front Psychol.* 9:4 (2013), 334. doi:10.3389/fpsyg.2013.00334

"A zebrafish can repair its own heart": G. Beffagna, "Zebrafish as a Smart Model to Understand Regeneration After Heart Injury: How Fish Could Help Humans," *Front Cardiovasc Med.* 6:107 (2019). doi:10.3389/fcvm.2019.00107

Acknowledgements

I'm so happy and grateful to be part of several incredible groups of writers, who have provided years of friendship and inspiration. Thank you to the People of LWON, and to our inimitable Ann Finkbeiner, who keeps us all relatively in line. Even though IJAB, your words and funny emails mean so much to me. More thanks to the writers of Scilance and Kendall Powell, who started it all, for many years of wisdom and wit. And fabulous, fabulist gratitude to the Cloudmakers/Fortune Cookie Collective for making beautiful new imaginary worlds when the one we were in seemed pretty dark.

Thank you to the editors who helped shape these essays. Your work and wisdom shine through every line: Julie H. Case, Heather Pringle, Jude Isabella, Abbigail N. Rosewood, Michelle Nijhuis, Rona Marech, Brigid Hains, and Kathleen Yale. Thank you to Debra Leigh Scott and Hidden River Press for your pandemic fortitude and your enduring support of these essays.

Like stars, there are more wonderful people in my life than I could ever count. Here are a just few of the many friends who've gone above and beyond to encourage me in writing and in life: Helen Fields, Christie Aschwanden, Kathi Rivers Shannon, Hilary Schaper, Kate Siber, Stephen Ornes, Elise McGuiness, Jayne Patterson, Trina Diaz, Chris Unno, Sarah Campe, and Gemme von Knopka. And my brightest points of light: Chris, Malachi, Flynn, and Seamus. I love you, and use your fork.

―――

In gratitude to the following publications, in which these essays found their original homes and original forms:

The Last Word On Nothing: Auditing Astronomy Class; View from Above; Window Seat; Lonely Abalone; Alligator Awesome; Small; Snail Season; June Gloom; In Warm Water; On Tap, Special Reserve; Rainbow Connection; Brave New Worlds; Egg Drop; Fruit Fly Walks into a Bar; What's My Lipstick?; Orchid Care for the Uncertain; Knight Moves; Yes, We Did; Loose Ends; Maybe More Than You Wanted To Know About Hearts

Hakai Magazine: The Sadness of Solving a Mystery; Psyche and the Seashore; If You Feed Them, They Will Come

Aeon: Moonstruck

Alaska Airlines Magazine: Grunion Run; Taking the High Road

High Country News: Depth Afield; Points of Light; Watching the Weather in California.

KQED: Flaming Pumpkins

National Parks Magazine: Landscape Poetry

Neon Door: Can 58,800+ Lights Help Us See What's Right In Front Of Us?

Orion: By-the-Wind Sailors

www.ingramcontent.com/pod-product-compliance
Lightning Source LLC
Chambersburg PA
CBHW021533150726
47990CB00006B/2221